This series offers the concerned reader basic guidelines and *practical* applications of religion for today's world. Although decidedly Christian in focus and emphasis, the series embraces all denominations and modes of Bible-based belief relevant to our lives today. All volumes in the Steeple series are originals, freshly written to provide a fresh perspective on current—and yet timeless—human dilemmas. This is a series for our times.

Among the books:

Woman in Despair: A Christian Guide to Self-Repair
Elizabeth Rice Handford

How to Read the Bible
James Fischer

Bible Solutions to Problems of Daily Living
James W. Steele

A Book of Devotions for Today's Woman
Frances Carroll

Temptation: How Christians Can Deal with It
Frances Carroll

With God on Your Side: A Guide to Finding Self-Worth Through Total Faith
Doug Manning

A Spiritual Handbook for Women
Dandi Daley Knorr

A Daily Key for Today's Christians: 365 Key Texts of the New Testament
William E. Bowles

Walking in the Garden: Inner Peace from the Flowers of God
Paula Connor

How to Bring up Children in the Catholic Faith
Carol and David Powell

Sex in the Bible: An Introduction to What the Scriptures Teach Us About Sexuality
Michael R. Cosby

How to Talk with God Every Day of the Year: A Book of Devotions for Twelve Positive Months
Frances Hunter

God's Conditions for Prosperity: How to Earn the Rewards of Christian Living
Charles Hunter

Help in Ages Past, Hope for Years to Come: Daily Devotions from the Old Testament
Robert L. Cate

Journey into the Light: Lessons of Pain and Joy to Renew Your Energy and Strengthen Your Faith
Dorris Blough Murdock

Prentice-Hall International, Inc., *London*
Prentice-Hall of Australia Pty. Limited, *Sydney*
Prentice-Hall Canada Inc., *Toronto*
Prentice-Hall of India Private Limited, *New Delhi*
Prentice-Hall of Japan, Inc., *Tokyo*
Prentice-Hall of Southeast Asia Pte. Ltd., *Singapore*
Whitehall Books Limited, *Wellington, New Zealand*
Editora Prentice-Hall do Brasil Ltda., *Rio de Janeiro*

PILGRIMAGES

A GUIDE TO THE HOLY PLACES OF EUROPE FOR TODAY'S TRAVELER

Paul Lambourne Higgins

A SPECTRUM BOOK

Prentice-Hall, Inc., Englewood Cliffs, New Jersey 07632

Library of Congress Cataloging in Publication Data

Higgins, Paul Lambourne.
    Pilgrimages, a guide to the holy places of Europe for today's traveler.

    (Steeple books)
    "A Spectrum Book."
    Includes index.
        1. Christian shrines—Europe—Guide-books.
    2. Christian pilgrims and pilgrimages—Europe.
    3. Europe—Description and travel—1971-   —Guide-books.   I. Title.   II. Series.
    BX2320.5.E85H53   1984   263'.042'4   83-17807
    ISBN 0-13-676163-1
    ISBN 0-13-676155-0 (pbk.)

To my wife, Ruth,
with love and gratitude

Chapter-opening ornaments reprinted from
Pictorial Archive of Printer's Ornaments from the Renaissance to the 20th Century,
selected by Carol Belanger Grafton (1980, Dover Publ. Inc., New York), p. 90.

1 2 3 4 5 6 7 8 9 10

ISBN 0-13-676163-1

ISBN 0-13-676155-0 {PBK.}

Editorial/production supervision by William P. O'Hearn
Cover design by Hal Siegel
Manufacturing buyer: Edward J. Ellis

CONTENTS

PREFACE

Certain places on the earth are believed to be charged with unusual spiritual power. Some, such as Chartres Cathedral in France or Glastonbury Abbey in England, are widely known as great shrines surrounded by centuries of history and legend. Other highly energized sites are known only to a few spiritual seekers.

The actual traveler with a spiritual interest and feeling for adventure, as well as the armchair traveler with similar tendencies, will find these power centers to be places of mystery and fascination.

It was Sir Thomas More, the famed sixteenth-century scholar and pilgrim, who said that "God wishes to be worshiped in particular places." There is certainly an amazing sense of blending of this world and the Other World at certain points on the surface of Mother Earth. Some specific places, such as holy wells and enchanted valleys, reflect a combination of pagan and Christian influences, often involving a contact with nature spirits and other orders of being. Certain sites may have first come to notice as a result of a visionary experience or as a place where people found healing. Sensitive persons become aware of the presence of spirits and angelic entities in some of these places.

Psychical investigators have culled most interesting evidences of unusual phenomena at many of the sites. Some point to "ley lines" of energy under the earth's surface, making for a pattern of spiritual meaning and harmony. Others see a combination of natural beauty and energy mingled with historic events and spirit entities as giving a certain place a special aura of attractiveness and power. Still others attribute the power to a blending of faith and prayer and the presence of unseen beings.

In this book we look at a number of sacred and enchanting sites in northern Europe where the spiritual powers are evident today. My wife and I have visited these places, and in them we have experienced spiritual manifestations of various types. I am particularly grateful for my wife's many suggestions relating our travel experiences to the purpose of the book and for her typing of the manuscript. Likewise appreciation is expressed for the valuable counsel of Kenneth and Margaret Sallenger, who accompanied us to some of these special sites.

The purpose of this guidebook is to point out a few of these sacred places in their ever-interesting and sometimes enthralling surroundings, with the expectation that each traveler will find an authentic joy in being on holy ground. In this spirit the delights of travel become a real part of a happy and fulfilling pilgrimage.

PILGRIMAGES

THE BRITISH ISLES

GLASTONBURY

From the earliest times Glastonbury has been a center for worship and a place of unusual sanctity to pagans and Christians alike. Many are the mysteries surrounding this area in Somerset: mysteries associated with the Druids and the old Gods, with the coming of Christianity, with King Arthur and the Fisher King, and with the quest for the Holy Grail.

This lovely scene, near the Mendip hills where the pyramidal Tor looms above the ancient ruins of the abbey, holds a perennial fascination for today's pilgrims as well as those of centuries past. There is, of course, more to Glastonbury than meets the eye. It has been called "the gateway to the Unseen." An acquaintance with its history and legend will help prepare one to appreciate what is probably the oldest lamp of Christianity in northern Europe. If one is sensitive to psychic vibrations, much more may be revealed.

Glastonbury has been often thought of as Avalon, the ancient Celtic Paradise, and a sort of New Jerusalem, where the spiritual world penetrates the material geographical area. It was an island at one time, before the silt from the River Severn produced the low-lying lands, filling in around the hills. No doubt the ancient center of worship took place on the Tor, the high point rising some 522 feet above sea level and from which height today one can get a marvelous view of Somerset. On the top of the Tor there still stands the tower of the old chapel dedicated to the Archangel Michael.

A strongly supported legend says that Saint Joseph of Arimathea, close friend or relative of the Lord Jesus, came to Glastonbury a few years after the Resurrection of Christ. Eleven followers accompanied him, and Saint Joseph is believed to have taken with him the sacred Chalice used at the Last Supper. He is reported to have had a dream in which an angel told him to go to that place near the southern English coast where there is a large hill resembling Mount Tabor in Galilee. When he saw the Tor, Saint Joseph knew he had come to the holy place. On nearby Wearyall Hill he thrust his staff into the ground, where it took root and lives to blossom every year on the holy thorns. Slips of the original continue to bloom; and it is said that the Glastonbury rose is not found anywhere else in Britain and that it is of the same species still found in Syria and Palestine. The pagan king granted these early Christians permission to settle at Avalon and even gave them the land. An angel visitant whom tradition says was the Archangel Gabriel told them to build a little chapel to the honor of the Blessed Virgin Mary. The little wattle church, built there in Glastonbury, was the first Christian edifice in Britain, and some historians believe it to be the first in Europe. The Christian work flourished for some years but fell into a decline in the second century, later to be restored by two missionaries. Known as the Old Church, or Saint Mary's Chapel, it became the center for pilgrimages until the great fire of 1184, when most of the medieval monastery buildings at Glastonbury were destroyed.

Saint Patrick and other holy men of the fifth century visited Glastonbury. Saint Bride, who was an avatar of the Celtic goddess Bridget, a guardian of the hearthside, and protector of women in childbirth, came and established her cell not far from Wearyall. Saint David, sixth-century patron saint of Wales, came with seven bishops to dedicate a new church to the Virgin. But he was told by Mary herself in a vision that her church was already dedicated to her because of the very sanctity of the ground. The Benedictine rule was established, and in time the great abbey was built.

Accounts of King Arthur's association with Glastonbury in the sixth century have interesting roots. The twelfth-century Giraldus Cambrensis writes of how some monks in 1191 discovered Arthur's grave, a grave that may be seen today. The Tor was called *insula Avallonia,* the Apple-isle, and Giraldus says it was ruled by the matron Morganis, a blood relative to King Arthur. Giraldus says she had taken Arthur after the battle of Kemelen to the place now called Glastonbury to heal his wounds.

The great theologian Saint Dunstan (909–988) was educated at Glastonbury and later served for some years as abbott, directing the rebuilding of the structures. The destruction of the abbey, which followed the dissolution of the monasteries in the 1540s and occurred during the revolution of the 1640s, was a tragic reminder of man's occasional insensitivity to spiritual values. The old spiritual powers, of course, remained, and mystics honored the hallowed grounds. The poet William Blake echoed the idea that even Christ as a child had been in England and had walked on that precious earth known today as Glastonbury.

In the earlier years of the twentieth century, the Church of England employed as curator of the abbey ruins Bligh Bond, well-known architect and restorer of old churches who used psychic methods in making some significant discoveries. Through a gifted psychic friend came communications from a monk of former times, telling of certain side-chapels and a chapel behind the sanctuary of which there had been no written records. Everything was found exactly as the old monk had described, with continuing discoveries made as, night after night, communications came through from several different spirit entities.

One legend holds that at one time the Chalice of Christ was on the altar of Saint Mary's Church, having been brought by Saint Joseph of Arimathea to Glastonbury. But, when dark times came to this "holyest earthe in England," the sacred relic was entrusted to the keeping of that mysterious agent of the higher realms, the Fisher King. He is believed to have kept it in his underground chambers in the heart of Chalice Hill, guarded by three pure maidens of supernormal strength. The continuing quest for the Holy Grail involves mysteries that relate to the inner experience of the soul.

Surely in a concrete and practical way there is some kind of relation between the grail legends and the effective presence of the Chalice Well at Glastonbury. The well is about a half mile from the abbey. The waters have been famed from early times for their healing properties. The spring, coming from an unknown subterranean source, has a constant flow of about a thousand gallons per hour, and it has never been known to fail, not even during severe droughts. The well structure consists of two chambers, one pentagonal, and may be of pre-Christian origin. The waters were used by the ancient religious groups, perhaps the Druids, and by Christians through the centuries for healing and sacerdotal purposes. In the mid-twentieth century the Chalice Well property was purchased by a group of Christians, headed by Major W. Tudor Pole. A trust was formed with the purpose "to preserve and safeguard forever the famous Spring and Well, and the surrounding gardens and orchard, as a site sacred to the memory of the first Christian missionaries to our island, a place from which the Christ Message was said to have been first proclaimed to the people of the Western World at the beginning of the Christian era."[1]

Glastonbury has so much to see; each surviving edifice or stone from the old abbey area seems to have a story of its own—the remains of the Lady Chapel and St. Joseph's Well, the Great Church, the Tithe Barn, the Abbot's Kitchen, St. Patrick's Chapel, and the Holy Thorn, King Arthur's Shrine, as well as the Tor, and the Chalice Well, and St. John's Church. Pilgrims today, as of yore, wend their way to Glastonbury to find not only quiet beauty but vital power and meaning breaking through from other dimensions.

[1] *The Origin and Purpose of the Chalice Well Trust* (Glastonbury, England: Chalice Well Trust, n.d.).

6

The lovely city of Bath makes a good center for sightseeing in the richly historic west country. With its Roman origins and ancient baths—the waters being long cherished for their therapeutic value and still widely used—Bath is an especially beautiful city. Bath Abbey itself is an architectural gem. The abbey's striking facade (with its sculptured stone of the ascending and descending angels of Jacob's ladder) and the exquisite windows and vaulted ceiling of the interior make the abbey a structure not to be missed. Then, too, the city has handsome Georgian crescent buildings and many reminders of famous visitors. John Wesley preached here often in the days when Beau Nash presided over the Pump Room.

According to one legend, Prince Bladud, father of King Lear, had been banished because of his leprosy. In his miserable state he had led his pigs from place to place until coming one day to a swampy marsh. There the leprous prince was healed in the warm waters rising from springs believed to be sacred. The place was soon found by others and was called Bath. The old chronicles tell how sick persons from all over England went to bathe in these healing waters. Monastic hospitals were established, and it was said that old people lived longer and healthier lives in Bath.

The main road that leads from Bath to Glastonbury goes through that idyllic cathedral city of Wells. The twelfth-century Gothic cathedral is one of the best loved in England, and a visitor cannot but be inspired in walking from the old Gate House (where a few charming rooms are available for lodging in the little inn that was built before America was discovered) across the lawns to the Cathedral, with its facade of the saints as welcoming celestial hosts. Inside the Cathedral are the famous inverted stone arches and that wonderful old clock where the knights in armor hold their tournament at the striking of every hour. One should see, too, the bishop's palace with its picturesque moat and the draw bridge, and the attendant swans that ring a bell for meal time. And it is all on the way to Glastonbury.

Glastonbury can be reached by train from Paddington Station in London to Bath, and then by coach via Wells on Road 39. By private car one can take the slower, more southerly roads from London, via the cathedral city of Salisbury, continuing through Frome and Shepton Mallet on Route 361 into Glastonbury. One feels the proximity to this "holyest erthe in Englande" as the Tor begins to loom on the horizon.

Bath is an ideal center for one who wishes to spend time in this historic area. It is not only close to Wells and Glastonbury, but is also close to the great port city of Bristol. The pleasant, old-fashioned Francis Hotel is well-located.

Wells, one of England's loveliest cathedral cities, is another center for sightseeing in Somerset. The Swan Hotel has foundations going back to 1410 and is a good place to lodge and dine. On the same street is the Ancient Gatehouse, with several rooms facing the cathedral. It is a small inn that is ancient indeed as well as charming and comfortable. One may have to stand on a footstool to get into the high canopied bed.

Glastonbury itself has the still popular little George and Pilgrim Inn, which dates to the fifteenth century.

CORNWALL

Cornwall, the ancient Celtic duchy occupying the southwest corner of England, is so rich in places of mystic connotation and psychic manifestations that each holy well or stone circle or medieval parish church could be a subject for serious study. The rugged coasts, the picturesque fishing villages, the streams and meadows, the pleasant climate all make Cornwall an attractive place for a holiday, as the English well know. But it is the pilgrim who is set on seeing spiritual power centers who finds unlimited opportunities in this land of the ancient giants and perennial mermaids, of witches and wizards, of Celtic saints and miracle-workers.

St. Michael's Mount, near Penzance, is one of the most beautiful sights on this southern coast. A small rock island, about a mile in circumference, it can be reached during low tide by a causeway. The isle, with its old monastery and castle, resembles the famous Mont St. Michel of Normandy, although Cornwall's is on a smaller scale. Legend has it that St. Michael, the great archangel, appeared on the summit of this isle in the fifth century and that this led to the building of the earliest chapel there. It has been a place of pilgrimage since the Middle Ages, and in recent years groups from the Churches' Fellowship for Psychical and Spiritual Studies have made their pilgrimages to St. Michael's Mount.

Tintagel, long associated with King Arthur, is a striking scene on the rugged northern Cornish coast. The medieval castle ruins, probably originally built over a much earlier fortress, are high above the sea and extend as a rocky precipice almost surrounded by the mighty waters. When four of us were visiting Tintagel on a bleak, windy, rainy day, it was not difficult to picture the immortal Merlin conjuring up the storm. Early Welsh songs identify the place with Arthur and Merlin, and threads of the ancient narratives are brought into the Arthurian stories of Lord Tennyson and R.S. Hawker.

Robert S. Hawker (1803–1875), of course, is one of the most delightful of all Cornish characters. Anglican priest, preacher, mystic, author, poet, occultist, and friend to shipwrecked sailors and the needy, he was for forty-one years the eccentric, lovable, and saintly rector of Morwenstow, with its beautiful old parish church and holy well on the northern coast. The church is named for St. Morwenna, who had a cell and baptistry near the cliff in the fifth century. Like other Celtic saints, she no doubt used the waters for healing purposes. Hawker writes that the ancient stone crosses were erected as guide posts on a straight line between the holy centers, rather like spirit paths that were originally traced by the feet of angels. He tells how these paths are linked with the flow of the seasons and that spirit-animated phallic stones combine with the maternal powers of Mother Earth in producing a variety of currents of fertility. Hawker's views are similar to those expressed in geomancy, that science or art that seeks to bring human habitation and activity into harmony with the visible and invisible world, showing magnetic-like spiritual lines on the earth's surface.

One of the loveliest churches of the west country is St. Neot's, beautifully situated on high ground. The Norman tower bears an oak branch as a perpetual reminder that during the dark days of the 1640s this parish was loyal to King Charles I. Every year on King Charles Day, a fresh oak branch is placed on the tower. Nearby is the famous holy well, where in olden times St. Neot would stand in the waters reciting the Scriptures and healing the sick. The well is amid a sylvan scene, and the foundations of it are very old, although retouched in the nineteenth century. On a visit to that ancient and lovely scene on a quiet sunny afternoon, while cattle and sheep grazed on the hillside, I seemed lifted into another dimension as I filled a vessel with water from the sacred well.

St. Neot lived in the ninth century and was a kinsman of King Alfred the Great. His early training was at Glastonbury Abbey, and he went to Cornwall for quiet retreat, forming a small monastery at the place now named for him. Neot was a very little man, believed to be hunchbacked, and he had to stand on a stool to say Mass. He was a great friend of the animals of the woods and always warned them when he heard of the approach of hunters. One day when his oxen were stolen by thieves, his friend the red deer came in from the forest and helped him plow. After he departed to the next world, St. Neot's body was taken by King Alfred into Huntingdonshire to a place now also called St. Neot's.

The waters of the holy well at St. Neot's in Cornwall and of various other wells in that area have been known for their curative powers from earliest times. St. Keyne, a fifth-century

Welsh princess known for both her beauty and her kindness, lived in her latter years in Cornwall and is reported to have had a close association with the water spirits. She could bring forth water from the ground and would then use the water for healing the sick. Another noted holy well, in a cave on the beach in Cubert, was long known for curing various children's diseases; other wells are associated with healing insanity, blindness, and sore eyes, and many types of sickness and wounds.

Of the many great standing stones in Cornwall, some are connected with magical and fertility rites. Some of the stone circles are considered by psychically gifted persons to be particularly charged with very strong energies. At a doughnut-shaped stone near St. Just, psychic powers for healing are thought to be present and experienced by one who enters the hole in the center. An outstanding megalith is the stone monument called the Zennor Quoit in the little coastal town of Zennor. It is known, too, for its mermaids and for the magic gifts of certain parishioners linked with its medieval church.

The coming of John Wesley (1703–1791), who made thirty-seven preaching tours through Cornwall, brought fresh spiritual power to the ancient duchy. Of the many healing experiences recorded in his monumental *Journal,* a number took place in Cornwall. When he preached to great throngs, especially large numbers came to hear him in Gwennap Pit, near Redruth, in the area's once-rich mining center. The famous pit may have been a part of an ancient mining operation or perhaps, as some believe, a place for early performing of the mysteries. Wesley first preached in the pit in 1762, its amphitheater design lending itself well to such a purpose. The venerable man of God preached there for the last time when he was eighty-five. Gwennap Pit is still used for festive religious gatherings, and if one traditional view is accepted it may well be one of the oldest spiritually oriented meeting places in England.

The story is told of one night when John Wesley, on one of his many visits to Cornwall, stayed at St. Agnes at an old haunted house. He was disturbed at midnight and found that the great hall was set for a banquet. Among those present was a gentleman with a red feather in his cap, who invited Wesley to join them. Taking a vacant chair, the preacher said that before eating he would ask a blessing. Upon his request, the company rose, but as Wesley pronounced the sacred words the room grew dark and the ghostly guests vanished.

The old Celtic mystic power persists in Cornwall: in the great stones and holy wells, and parish churches, in the fertility lines both visible and invisible, in the varied influences from the Druids to the Wesleyans, and on the rocky coasts and the inland moors.

Tips for Travelers

Train service from London's Paddington station is good to Plymouth, Truro, and Penzance. At Bodmin Road there is a junction for Bodmin. Also, motor coach service runs to Bodmin.

Bodmin, being somewhat in the center of the ancient duchy of Cornwall, is a convenient place for lodging, especially for one with a car available. Castle Hill House, a late Georgian residence on the northeast outskirts of town, is recommended by the British Travel Authority. The fifteenth-century St. Petroc's Church, one of the largest in Cornwall, and its holy well are in Bodmin.

St. Neot's is a drive of about eight miles directly west of Bodmin. With a car one can make a thrilling all-day trip from Bodmin, going east to Truro, where the lovely late nineteenth-century cathedral can be visited, and then to Gwennap Pit (three miles south of Redruth). About twenty miles beyond is Penzance, with its Gilbert and Sullivan reminders and with St. Michael's Mount. Further west is Land's End, and on the coastal route circling to the north is the old magical area of the mermaids of Zennor and St. Ives and its beautiful bay.

Another fascinating journey from Bodmin is to drive northeast through Camelford to Tintagel, the old King Arthur Castle, and a few miles beyond Bude to historic Morwenstow.

The cathedral city of Truro would make another good base for visiting Cornwall. Of course, the seaside towns are especially lovely, but they are crowded in summer months and are generally more expensive.

THE HOLY ISLAND

In the most northerly part of England, not far from the Scottish border, is ancient Lindisfarne. North of Hadrian's Wall, built by the first-century Roman emperor, the country near the shores of the North Sea bears marks of one of the most important periods of early Christian history. In many ways it is an unspoiled area, and miles of the Northumberland landscape have not changed much with the passing of the centuries. Just off that northeastern coast are several islands known as the Farnes, and the largest of the group has long been known as Lindisfarne. More often than not it is called the Holy Island.

Lindis is the name of the tidewater one must cross to reach the island, and *farne* is from the word *fahren,* which means a recess or place of retreat. The island is accessible by a causeway during low tide, but it is cut off from the mainland for a few hours twice a day during high tide. In early times great poles were located between the mainland and the Holy Island so pilgrims caught in a rising tide could climb a pole and keep dry and safe until the tide receded.

In 635 Saint Aidan, a monk in the monastery on the Isle of Iona, went to Lindisfarne with the Gospel. He formed the monastery there and trained English boys in such a way that they had a great influence for good throughout the north country. Bishop Aidan followed the policy of not allowing any accumulation of wealth, but rather immediately putting into use all surplus for freeing slaves and meeting the needs of the poor. In his religious and humane work he had the support of good King Oswald. St. Aidan followed the old Celtic liturgical ways rather than those customarily followed by the western church. The early thatched church and other buildings erected in Aidan's time were later destroyed by Danish invaders. A statue of the early saint may be seen near the village center on the Holy Island.

The Venerable Bede (673-735), father of English historians and whose writings, *The Ecclesiastical History of the English People* and *The Life and Miracles of St.Cuthbert,* are among the most fascinating of all classics, tells of an interesting event. One night a young devout shepherd watching his sheep along the hills near the seacoast saw a most amazing phenomenon. He beheld some angels carrying the beloved bishop to heaven. The next day the shepherd boy learned that Bishop Aidan had died during the night. So impressed was he with this visionary experience that he decided to begin monastic studies. His name was Cuthbert, and he became one of the greatest spiritual men in England's history, one especially revered for his purity of life, his helpfulness to the poor, his healing the sick, and his friendship with the birds and animals. St. Cuthbert in his latter years lived a hermit's life at his retreat on the tiny island of Farne, where he gave himself to healing prayers and is known to have learned the language of the birds. His body was buried on Lindisfarne. Later, when the Viking raids began, the monks took his coffin with the bones to the mainland. They carried these relics from place to place for two hundred years, until they were placed in Durham Cathedral. St. Cuthbert's wooden coffin, with its carved figure of the Virgin Mary on the side of it, may be seen today at Durham, where a fine stained glass window honors this sainted miracle-worker. Bede's shrine, with four great candlesticks, may also be seen at the great Norman Cathedral in Durham.

An eleventh-century Norman Church was built in Lindisfarne and the mission flourished again. Remnants of the ancient priory may be seen, and on top of a rocky crag overlooking the North Sea is a picturesque sixteenth-century castle. On visits to the Holy Island I have felt the permeating blessing of those good and great souls, St. Aidan and St. Cuthbert, and all the others in a long line of faithful service. Likewise one is reminded of the famous Lindisfarne Gospels, magnificently copied and illuminated by two Holy Island bishops about 724 and now constituting one of the major treasures of the British Museum in London.

Tips for Travelers

A few miles south of the Scottish-English border in Northumberland, on Route 1, a road turns off to Beal, continuing to the shore of the North Sea and the Holy Island of Lindisfarne. The causeway to the island is passable by car or coach during low tide. Travelers should learn in advance the hours of the tides.

Bamburgh, a fine castle town a few miles south of the Holy Island, is a place one might stay. A bed and breakfast stop in a Northumberland village or farmhouse can be delightful. If Edinburgh is one's center, Lindisfarne would be a good day's round trip by car.

LINCOLN

Lincoln has had a Christian community since Roman times. The present cathedral, built over an earlier structure, is one of the most magnificent monuments to God in northern Europe, and is unrivalled in all England for its majestic position on a great hill. The imposing structure can be seen for miles around, a wondrous example of architectural splendor. The radiant beauty of the great western facade takes on a transcendent quality at sunset that cannot be soon forgotten. Standing before it is like being at the entry to a veritable fairyland. This remarkably wide facade with its carved saints is like an embodiment of an encompassing cloud of witnesses.

After the fire and earthquake of 1185, St. Hugh, Bishop of

Lincoln, soon started the new structure and dedicated it to Our Lady Saint Mary. The great bell tower, one of the most handsome in the world, and the other towers reflect the strength of aspirations upward. The whole pile of marvelous stone is like a mighty rock connecting earth with heaven. Some beautiful thirteenth-century glass is located in the transept, and every foot of the interior, with its altars and vaulted ceilings and shrines, is filled with beauty. The church also has the famous Angel Choir and the mischievous imp that was turned to stone so long ago.

St. Hugh, one of the noblest saints of history whose spirit still influences the pilgrim who comes to this holy place, was a great champion of the poor and a worker for peace in Europe. He refused to pay taxes to Richard the Lion Hearted for wars against France, saying it was evil for Christian monarchs to be at war. In his courageous stand he asked all the people of his diocese in Lincolnshire to do likewise. When the lion-hearted king came with his soldiers to Lincoln to force the issue, St. Hugh had the cathedral bells rung, calling all his people to ascend the hillsides. Then he went out upon the steps to meet the king. The latter melted in the presence of the saintly bishop and gave Hugh a kiss of peace.

The shrines include those of St. Hugh himself, his grave being somewhere near the Angel Choir, of Little Saint Hugh, a youth who was murdered for his faith, of Robert Grosseteste, a great thirteenth-century bishop, scholar, and holy man, and of the fourteenth-century sainted bishop John Dalderby. All have been scenes of pilgrimages, and many healings have taken place. The whole cathedral is filled with vibrations of spiritual power. One time a dear friend in our travel group had been very ill. I took her to one of the altars at Lincoln and asked for the prayers of St. Hugh, the healing blessings of Our Lady and Our Lord. The woman was so much improved that day that she could enjoy the rest of our tour.

In the fall of 1978 while taking a picture in the nave, my good friend Irene Hughes, distinguished psychic from Chicago, said she felt strongly the presence of many spirit entities while standing by my side. When that film was developed, there appeared on the picture a translucent spirit form in the aisle just a few feet in front of the camera.

In the summer of 1982, when my wife and I had brought a group to see Lincoln Cathedral, I went to the old shrine of Robert Grosseteste for prayer. Then I walked to the Angel Choir area near the shrine of St. Hugh, and while standing viewing the beauty of the place, I suddenly felt myself strongly swaying back and forth. I knew from the experience that I was receiving a blessing from a dear spirit. A little while later in another part of the cathedral, I met one of the members of our group, Diana Finley, who told me with great feeling that she had just come from the area of St. Hugh's shrine. While there she had suddenly felt herself "weaving back and forth." Then I related my similar experience, and we agreed that St. Hugh or another kindred spirit was greeting us. I was to learn that Diana was gifted in psychical communication; later on our journey we shared several other evidential experiences.

Statues of Eleanora of Castile and Edward I appear at the front of the cathedral. Eleanora had married the king in accordance with a prophetic astrological prediction at the very hour of the day foretold, and the marriage was a happy one. When on the Crusades with her husband, she was unafraid of death, saying it is no farther from Syria to heaven than from England to heaven. When she died in Lincolnshire in 1290, a procession to London was made in thirteen days, with a cross erected at each night's stop, all the way to Charing Cross. It was the age of faith for queens and peasants alike, and the power of the enduring things of the Spirit remain radiantly present, both visibly and invisibly, in the Cathedral of Our Lady at Lincoln.

Through the centuries fogs have frequently covered Lincoln, and these climatic conditions made the area unpleasant for some people. In World War II people prayed that their lovely city and its great cathedral be spared from bombing. At the time when the worst air raids came to eastern England, fogs gathered over Lincoln, making the place invisible. The bombs never fell, and the thankful local folk complained no more about the fog.

Tips for Travelers

Lincoln can be reached by train from King's Cross Station in London in less than three hours. By car one could take M1 to Leicester and then could drive north on 46 into Lincoln.

The White Hart Hotel, for 700 years a hostelry of old Lincoln, is today a handsome and largely modern structure that preserves the traditional decor and atmosphere. Some of the rooms have splendid views of the magnificent cathedral, the sight of its illumined beauty at night being a memorable experience. The hotel is perfectly located less than a block from the cathedral and an equally short distance from the castle.

EPWORTH

Within thirty miles of Lincoln is the little town of Epworth—the ancient capital of the Isle of Axholme and the home of the Wesleys. In early times this section of Lincolnshire, a land of fens and marshes, was surrounded by waters and was known as an island. Then Dutch engineers drained it, with the support of the crown, and the topography was changed. In the southern end of Axholme in the early seventeenth century lived religious separatists, some of whom became the Pilgrim fathers who later sailed to the new world. In 1696 Samuel Wesley became rector of historic St. Andrew's Church at Epworth. He and his wife, the remarkable Susanna, were the parents of nineteen children, including John, the great founder of Methodism, and Charles, the most prolific hymn writer of history. Both John and Charles were baptized in the twelfth-century Norman parish church. In the adjoining graveyard is Samuel Wesley's tomb, upon which in later years John Wesley stood to preach to a great throng of people when the church doors of his early boyhood were closed to him.

Near the church is the famous Old Rectory, built upon the ruins of the one largely destroyed by the fire of 1709, when little John was rescued as a "brand plucked from the burning." A noted ghost, often called "Old Jeffrey," was a strange visitor to the rectory during the winter of 1716. The noises and activities were so bold and persistent that every person who witnessed them believed them to be supernormal. These events had an influence on John Wesley's subsequent life-long psychical investigations, so carefully recorded through the years in his remarkable *Journal,* which is the largest autobiographical work in the English language. He believed such experiences to be relevant in offering evidence regarding life after death and in support of a spiritual interpretation of life.

When the Old Rectory was restored in 1956, W. Le Cato Edwards, the warden and former missionary to India, sought to blend its historic significance with a new emphasis on religious retreats. In this way he helped to awaken the consciousness of serious travelers and pilgrims to the reality of a living shrine geared to spiritual renewal. The old Wesleyan spirit in men like Edwards triumphed over earlier obstacles, so that the very ground from which sprang the greatest spiritual revival of British history is recognized anew as a vital power center today.

Tips for Travelers

Epworth can be reached by car from Lincoln, via the old market town of Gainsborough on the River Trent, or from Doncaster. Train service to Doncaster from King's Cross in London is good. If one has made reservations to stay overnight at the Old Rectory, advance arrangements should also be made to be met by car at the Doncaster station.

For information regarding lodging, write the Warden,

The Old Rectory, Epworth, Doncaster, So. Yorkshire, England
DN9 1HB.

LONDON

London holds a universal interest, so manifold are the fascinating and historic aspects of its long life and so widespread its influence throughout the world. The great author of the dictionary and one of the most celebrated of all Londoners, Dr. Samuel Johnson (1709–1784), once commented, "When a man is tired of London, he is tired of life; for there is in London all that life can afford."[2]

No doubt there has been a settlement at what is now called London for many millenia, going back centuries before Christ. While historic records, according to Tacitus, tell of Londinium in the earlier years of the first century before Christ and mention the struggles between the Romans and Queen Boadicea, whose great statue stands at Westminster Bridge, legendary accounts as well as excavations indicate a much earlier history. The changing scenes of the past twenty centuries are well-known, and the importance of London as a major city since the days of Alfred the Great is an absorbing story.

Spiritual energies associated with both pre-Christian and Christian traditions in London make it a very powerful mystical center. Elusive indeed are these energies amid so great a population and among so many who seem insensitive to such. Yet the spiritual powers are present and effective.

The most famous monuments in Greater London, although not the oldest nor necessarily the most powerful spiritual centers, are Westminster Abbey and St. Paul's Cathedral.

In very early times the Isle of Thorns was in the River

---

[2]James Boswell, *Life of Samuel Johnson*, The Modern Library (New York: Random House, n.d.), p. 733.

Thames, and it was considered a holy place, becoming the site of the first Abbey Church. Tradition indicates a church was built there around 616 by King Sebert of Essex, and a Benedictine community was established. Edward the Confessor started reconstruction of the old church around 1050, and it was consecrated in 1065. The ground was holy ground indeed, and all English monarchs since William I were crowned there. Some of their graves are at Westminster Abbey, too, as are the tombs of such great poets as Chaucer, Browning, and Tennyson. Edward the Confessor's shrine has for centuries been a central place of devotion. Edward's Chair, used by the monarchs at the coronation, was designed to contain the famous relic known as the Stone of Scone, which forms its seat. Many legends surround the Stone. Some contend it was the stone on which Jacob laid his head at Bethel. It has been moved from place to place, tradition claiming it was used in Spain, at Tara in Ireland, for St. Columba at Iona, and for the early Scottish kings.

Some believe that people practiced religious worship on the abbey grounds long before the introduction of Christianity. On the south side of the cloisters are ancient graves. "Long Meg," the semi-mythical giantess and wonder-worker of the Lake Country in early Britain who is celebrated by a great monolith stone circle near Penrith in Cumberland, has her grave in this cloister area, according to the old accounts.

St. Paul's Cathedral, the great masterwork of Sir Christopher Wren built after the 1666 fire of London, stands on the site of former structures going back to the seventh century. A tradition says that a Roman temple stood on this site at the head of Ludgate Hill.

Not until after the bombs dropped on St. Bride's Church on December 29, 1940, did the antiquity of that site come to light. The destruction of all but the tower of the famed Christopher Wren building on Fleet Street, the popular church of the journalists and the literary men, was followed by a clearing away of the debris and a discovery of vast underground structures of early Roman times. Excavations revealed more than a thousand years of hidden history, showing that St. Bride's spans the whole development of Christianity in Britain and is linked with religious worship there long before Christ.

Built near the River Thames above an important holy well, the church was no doubt the site of religious worship in the Roman era. Some scholars believe that God, under one name or another, has been worshipped there for at least 3000 years. A mysterious second-century building has been found in the excavation, and this could have been one of the early Christian churches. A church stood there in the sixth century, named in honor of St. Bridget of Ireland (born A.D. 453), called St. Bride. It was a Celtic church, not too closely related to the Roman Church in those days, and some believe that St. Bridget herself visited the place or at least came in visionary form. She is often associated with the ancient Celtic Goddess Keridwen, reflecting a sort of blending of pagan and Christian virtues, an inspirer of poetry, culture, and humane values.

The later history of St. Bride's is well-known but takes on a new richness of meaning because of the excavations. The edifice was an important structure when King John held his Parliament there in 1210. The first printing press in England was alongside St. Bride's. After the Great Fire of 1666, Wren helped to rebuild the church. His splendid tower, tiered like a wedding cake, stood alone after the 1940 destruction. The church has been beautifully rebuilt and was rededicated in 1957, with Queen Elizabeth II present. The black marble on the floor came from Belgium and the white marble from Italy. With the magnificent vaulted ceiling, the church is a lovely place indeed made even more conducive to worship with its great organ and choirs. Today's pilgrim will find St. Bride's a true place for quiet moments amid the rush of the outer streets. Pilgrims will be especially excited to go below and see the well marked and lighted excavations and then to pause quietly for a bit at the old reopened underground chapel.

St. Peter-Upon-Cornhill, standing on the highest point in the old city, has foundations reputed to go back to A.D. 179, and by 700 was known as London's oldest church. The present structure is probably the fifth on this ancient site of worship. A short distance away is the Church of St. Michael, Cornhill, which dates to before the Norman Conquest. But the church has other associations, such as its proximity to a well found nearby and an ancient Roman wall, that may indicate earlier religious worship. A ministry of healing is fostered there today. To walk another couple of blocks in this most fascinating part of the city is to see St. Katharine Cree Church on Leadenhall Street. The church is chiefly associated with King Charles I, whose memory is revered in the richly decorated banner of the Society of King Charles the Martyr and in the restored chapel, where its fine wood carving of the great monarch who practiced "the king's touch" in the healing of the sick still shines. The present structure, consecrated by Archbishop William Laud in 1630, is a successor of the much earlier church that was an outpost of a twelfth-century priory.

A very potent spiritual center of great antiquity is on Ely Place in Holborn. St. Etheldreda's Church is the first pre-Reformation shrine restored to the Roman Church in England. Once a large complex of buildings, all rich in history, was there, but only the church survives. Shakespeare tells of John of Gaunt and Richard II being there, and Anne of Denmark writes of hearing the great Bishop Thomas Ken preaching in the sanctuary. The present structure, begun in 1291, survived the great fire, but the earlier building dates to the fourth century.

When I went to the rather unimposing church and knocked for admission, I felt like a psychic communication was already established when the door was opened immediately by a priest who sensed why we had come. At once he suggested we go to the crypt, the masonry of which he dated to A.D. 310. The crypt, with its distinctive character, is a remarkable place for prayer, the spiritual vibrations being unusually strong. The ancient rugged walls of stone, eight feet thick, and the heavy blackened timbers seem themselves to be impregnated with the calming power of the continuing centuries. The ground is hallowed, and just beyond the wall under the present street is the holy well, which in the old days was used for healing, the waters being especially efficacious for both people and cattle. The cross of St. Andrew was used in the blessing and healing acts.

The sanctuary above is lovely, with its fine east window portraying Christ with the Virgin Mother and St. Joseph, St. Etheldreda, St. Bridgit, and the Four Evangelists, but the great power comes from the crypt chapel below. St. Etheldreda, born to a royal family of Sussex in about 630, founded a monastery at Ely and after her death became particularly known for her intercessory healing.

A number of other very old churches in London—St. Bartholemew's, Great St. Helen's, and St. Mary-le-Bow, to name a few—have historic origins and associations of a supernormal character. Services of healing are held regularly at St. Mary Abchurch, a fourteenth-century church near The Bank of England, where the Churches' Fellowship for Psychical and Spiritual Studies has its London office. Spiritual undercurrents could well link some of these places, for a strange and often similar energy is felt in these churches quite different from that found in other religious edifices.

Of quite a different nature is the famed circular Temple Church not far from the law courts off Fleet Street. Taking its name from the Order of the Knights Templars, which was the order that gave protection to pilgrims journeying to Jerusalem, the round church near the banks of the Thames was built in the twelfth century. It had been consecrated to Mary by the Patriarch of Jerusalem. The church building contains medieval effigies, including the mysterious cross-legged figures, which some believe to be crusaders or perhaps Templars. After the dissolution of the Templars in 1312, the Knights Hospitallers took control of the Temple Church. The real purpose of the Templars remains a mystery. Whether St. Bernard had a role in the founding of the Knights Templars is still a question, and just how they were aligned with the unseen powers is another mystery. This is an interesting place to visit, but the vibrations there are mixed and perhaps unduly colored by influences of later history.

Out on London's City Road, in a commercial and semi-factory area, is a great spiritual power center where energies come forth in the more modern age in a way that gives it an authentic character like that of a new dispensation.

About two blocks west of Finsbury Circle are two of the most important places in London's long history. On one side of City Road are the old nonconformist Christian burial grounds known as Bunhill Fields, and immediately across the street is John Wesley's Chapel. The graves of Daniel Defoe, author of *Robinson Crusoe*; John Bunyan, author of *Pilgrim's Progress*; Isaac Watts, the revered hymn writer and Protestant divine; Susanna Wesley, the amazing mother of the Wesleys, and William Blake, the great poet, artist, mystic, and denizen of several worlds, are among those found there. Adjoining the fields is a common burial ground of the Quakers, where the bones of George Fox and his friends rest.

Wesley's Chapel was erected in 1778 and became a center for the Methodist societies in the latter years of John Wesley's life. When not on his frequent travels to every corner and town and hillside of Britain, the great man would preach there, too, and in later generations the sizable chapel became a major shrine and place of worship and service. The graves of John Wesley and many of his early preachers are in a little garden at the rear of the chapel. During World War II, Wesley's Chapel was untouched by bombs, although buildings on both sides were either leveled or badly damaged. In 1978, the handsome edifice, after a major renovation directed by the Pastor N. Allen Birtwhistle, was rededicated in the presence of Queen Elizabeth II and religious representatives from every continent. Next to the chapel is Wesley's house, where he stayed when in London and where on 2 March 1791 he died, saying "the best of all is, God is with us." The house, recently renovated, contains many treasures of Wesleyan interest, including his robe, spectacles, books, letters, and even the electrical machine he invented for healing purposes. The very small prayer room reflects a particularly vibrant aura. Wesley Chapel is a modern power center and is very much alive today.

Tips for Travelers

The London transportation system, with trains, both surface and underground, with motor coaches including the noted double-decker buses, and with the ever-present cabs, is perhaps the best in the world. A detailed map is helpful in finding one's way in this most fascinating metropolis, which consists of an amazing variety of historic communities. Even with the excellent public transportation, walking still remains an important way of reaching some of the sites and is essential for absorbing atmosphere that so radically changes from one borough or section to another.

The area of Russell Square and the British Museum, with one of the world's greatest collections of civilization's treasures, makes a good center for seeing some of the holy places of London. By taking Southampton Row and Kingsway to Aldwych and Fleet Street, one can soon be in the area of historic churches, such as the Temple, St. Bride's, and St. Paul's Cathedral. A bit further east are such ancient landmarks on Cornhill as St. Michael's and St. Peter's. In twenty to thirty minutes one can walk from Russell Square to Holborn Circus, just off of which is historic Ely Place and St. Etheldreda's Church.

The Russell Hotel, with its Victorian elegance, is splendidly situated at Russell Square. It is but three blocks from the British Museum, and only a block from the Russell Square underground station where there is a direct train to and from Heathrow Airport. Across the street from the Russell is the President Hotel, a little less expensive and very comfortable.

Travel companies in London offer many excellent one-day motor coach tours from London. One tour runs via Oxford to

Stratford-upon-Avon, giving a bit of the flavor of the Shakespeare landmarks. Tours also run to Windsor Castle and haunted Hampton Court, to Canterbury, and to Cambridge and Ely. One popular all-day excursion offers brief but interesting visits to Winchester and Salisbury Cathedrals, two of England's finest, as well as to Stonehenge.

An especially pleasant trip is to nearby St. Albans, for which one takes the train from the picturesque old St. Pancras railroad station. St. Albans dates from Roman times, and the great cathedral, with its exceptionally long nave, has the restored Shrine of St. Alban, England's first Christian martyr. St. Albans has very interesting excavations of the first-century Roman community.

IONA

"Behold Iona! A Blessing on each eye that see-eth it." These words of St. Columba, who arrived at the holy island in A.D. 563, are as true today as then. Off the rugged western Scottish coast, Iona is but three miles in length. It may be reached in one of two ways: by boat from Oban in about three hours, or by ferry to the island of Mull, then over the narrow roads for some twenty miles to Fionnphort for a one-mile open-boat crossing to the tiny Iona wharf.

St. Columba had come to this isle from Ireland with twelve disciples to spread the Gospel to the Scots. He was born in county Donegal in 521, a descendant of the early kings, and was ordained in the old Celtic Church. Upon arriving at Iona, he knew it was a holy place. Not wanting to look back toward his old homeland, he settled on the eastern shore where his eyes could see a new world for his labors. With the cold waters of the Atlantic beating upon the shores, he built a small hut over the stone that served as his bed. Iona became the chief lamp of Christianity in the north of Britain. For thirty-four years

Columba worked and prayed, practicing the healing of soul and body, going to the other islands and the mainland of Scotland with his message. He accomplished scholarly work, including the famous Book of Kells, the beautiful illuminated Gospels, and many other translations and original writings. Scottish kings came to the isle on pilgrimage during the great era when Iona's light was bright and far-reaching.

A great period of spiritual renewal followed, bringing hope and wholeness to the generations that built Christian values into the emerging civilization. In later centuries the isle declined in its influence, being ravaged by Viking raiders and pirates. But the spirit penetrating that holy place was never lost. While the abbey that was later built was dismantled in 1561 and the isle became primarily a grazing place for sheep and cattle, the dedicated work of those indefatigable holy men of the early period continued to shed an influence for good and to inspire many throughout Scotland and England.

Around 1640 devout King Charles I, eager to see the restoration of Iona to its former glory, made a grant urging the repair of the Cathedral Church but the Civil War came and the work could not be done. Not until 1899 did the Eighth Duke of Argyll give Iona Abbey in trust to the Church of Scotland, with this clear provision that "any recognized Christian denomination can apply for its use for the celebration of its full office of worship." A restoration program was inaugurated, and in 1938 the Iona Community was founded by the Reverend George MacLeod, distinguished Scottish churchman and spiritual leader. Lord MacLeod directed religious retreats with people coming from throughout Britain and other parts of the world to participate in the physical rebuilding of the abbey and in spiritual discipline and prayer. Spiritual healing and cooperative work for world peace are among the major concerns of the Iona Community, which consists of both a permanent and visiting religious community of clergy and laypersons.

It would seem that at long last St. Columba's prophecy is being fulfilled:

"In Iona of my heart, Iona of my love,
  Instead of monks' voices shall be lowing of cattle,
  But ere the world come to an end
  Iona shall be as it was."

The pilgrim who visits Iona, if only for an hour or two or for several days, will feel the spiritual power surrounding this most sacred island. The Abbey Church of St. Mary, so marvelously restored, is a vital place, filled with prayer and good activity. The old and new blend with the spirit of the eternal dimensions. St. Columba's shrine, the little chapel at the west entry, is believed to be over the ground where the holy man's relics are invisibly kept and has been restored. A few minutes of prayer in this sacred cell refreshes the spirit. At various places in the church visitors can feel the presence of the encompassing cloud of witnesses. St. Oran's Chapel should be visited, too. The beautifully carved Celtic Crosses, made of stone, are fascinating to see. St. Martin's cross, one of the finest in existence, dates to the tenth century. The circle around the arms of the cross represents eternal life. The island has many graves, including those of forty-eight Scottish kings, four Irish kings, and eight Norwegian monarchs. But far more in evidence are the living spirits of the saints, both of old and of today.

The Iona spirit has an inclusiveness and universality and an absence of any narrowness of view. Iona also has reminders of the old pre-Christian religion, one tradition referring to Iona as "the isle of the Druids." Perhaps this ancient influence is seen in the "tree of life" or "apis of the world" symbols on the Celtic crosses and elsewhere. Then, too, a holy well is used for healing and for renewal of youth "like the eagle's," and the island has Sithean Mor, and Great Fairy Mound. Once Columba was seen praying there, surrounded by flying angels. The "little people" are a part of the Iona heritage, too.

Sabine Baring-Gould, the British clergyman, writer, and antiquarian, records in his monumental *Lives of the Saints* some of the earliest and most authentic writings of Christian history in Britain. He tells how there came to St. Columba, shortly before his death in 597, the old white horse that had long carried milk to the monastery. The old horse, looking tearful, nuzzled him lovingly as Columba said to his friend, Diarmed, "leave him with me; let him weep for my departure. The Creator has revealed to this poor animal what He has hidden from thee." The old holy man caressed the horse and gave him a last blessing. When this was done he climbed upon a hilloch and looking over the holy island, pronounced his last prophecy: "Unto this place, albeit so small and poor, great homage shall yet be paid, not only by the kings and peoples of the Scots, but by the rulers of barbarous and distant nations with their people also. In great veneration too, shall it be held by the holy men of other churches."[3]

With a passionate love for traveling, St. Columba crossed the highlands to the north and east and visited the many islands. According to one tradition, he founded some 300 monastic centers in Scotland and northern England. In his little skiff, he was probably the first Christian to traverse Loch Ness and the river issuing from it. In those northern climes he won the friendship of King Brude and baptized many. He is said to have met the angels along the shores of Loch Ness. Being clairvoyant, Columba was able to see angelic and spirit entities. Sometimes an aged highlander would be carried to him for baptism, and Columba would describe the angels he could see carrying the departed soul to paradise. Accounts also tell of his experiences with the water monsters. Once in 565, when visiting Loch Ness, he rescued a person from possible danger by making the sign of the cross toward the monster, the latter at once retreating. On another occasion he is believed to have communicated with a monster, taming it, so that it became quite friendly. Since those early times water monsters have been sighted countless times in Loch Ness. No doubt a number of such creatures inhabit those northern waters today, as they have been seen and described by

[3]Sabine Baring-Gould, *The Lives of the Saints*, rev. ed. in 16 vols. (London: John C. Nimmo, 1908) 6:125.

reliable persons, including scientific investigators and Benedictine monks. The great creatures, said to range from fifteen to sixty feet in length, reflect another phase of life linked with mystery and touched by the spirit of St. Columba of Iona.

Tips for Travelers

Oban, in Argyll, is the ideal center for seeing western Scotland and for visiting the sacred isle of Iona. From the airport at Prestwick, coaches go to Glasgow, northward along the shores of Loch Lomond on Route 82 to Tyndrum and then on 85 to the Oban area.

From Oban one has two ways of reaching Iona. One is to take the 8:30 a.m. boat, which circles the Island of Mull, passes legendary Staffa, and either docks or sends a tender ashore at Iona, depending on weather conditions. After a couple of hours at Iona, the boat sails around the southern shores of Mull and across the Firth of Lorne, arriving at Oban about 6 p.m. The other way of reaching Iona is to take the ferry from Oban to Craignure, on Mull, and then a motor coach for some twenty miles or more on narrow roads to Fionnphort for the short boat trip across the Atlantic waters to holy Iona. If one wants to stay longer on Iona, one should write in advance to The Iona Community, Isle of Iona, Scotland, and arrange for lodgings on the island.

In Oban, the lovely Victorian style Alexandra Hotel faces the ocean. The front rooms provide especially good views of the harbor and the isles of the Firth. The food, with a fine and varied buffet, is very good.

ST. DAVID'S

The old Celtic tradition is still in evidence in Wales, and among the mountains and valleys, and along the sea coasts and freshwater streams persist reminders of the old legends. Modern

Druids and friends of the fairy world live in the Wales of today. Wales has the perennial goddesses, too, although their names are partially changed. The early Christian missionaries, wiser than many later ones, respected the old deities, accepting many of their rituals and ways and blending them with their faith in Jesus and Mary. The Goddess Bridget, important in Celtic lore, became associated in name and in healing powers with the late fifth-century Saint Bridget, whose feast day became February 1, and who in early writings is called the Prophetess of Christ. Many churches in the Celtic world are named for her, and in England she is known as St. Bride. Another favorite goddess in Wales is Rhiannon, known as the "Great Queen," who rides on a magic mare, her spirit blending with the animal and the foal. Her home is believed to be near a magical mound at St. Bride's Bay. Then there is the ever-present and mysterious Morgan le Fay, sometimes called the Queen of the Fairies and the Lady of the Lake, who appears in the wide range of Celtic mythology from Wales to the Alps. Sometimes King Arthur has been called her brother, and she is the one who carried Merlin away to an invisible world that interpenetrates this one.

St. David is no stranger to these traditions. The great and historic sixth-century Christian Patron of Wales, Dewi, or David, was born about 446 at Mynyw, the place now called St. David's. He died in 544 at the age of 98. It is said that his birth was predicted to his father years earlier in an unusual dream. David's mother, canonized by the Welsh and known as St. Non, was a healer and miracle-worker, whose holy well is near the bay, a couple of miles from the cathedral. As a youth, David studied in the magical area of the Black Mountains and dwelt along the Honddu River, when he was advised by an angel to found a monastery at his birthplace, the site of the present cathedral in Pembrokeshire.

St. David, much given to solitude and prayer, did not care much for ecclesiastical synods, and even in his founding of monastic centers he avoided unnecessary meetings. Ascetic in personal habits, he drank only water and abstained from animal food. Eloquent in preaching, he loved to worship and proclaim the Word. His emblem is a snow-white dove, seen in pictures perched on the saint's shoulder. It is said the bird had been sent from Heaven, and the dove and David talked together and joined their voices in singing hymns. Historic records attest to St. David's friendship with animals, including bees, with whom he worked to supply honey for the poor. Healing the sick and opening fountains of water in dry places, indicating perhaps his knowledge of ley lines, are characteristics of St. David's work. He conversed with the angels and had numerous visionary and prophetic experiences, even predicting the exact day of his death.

The cathedral bearing his name has been the major pilgrimage center of Wales for almost fourteen centuries. Much of the beautiful present structure, built of purple stone from the local quarries and somewhat hidden from the nearby sea coast by small rising hills that give it protection from pirates, dates to the twelfth century. It is a fascinating place to see, with the interesting tower ceilings, the blending of wood and stone, and the lovely Chapel of the Virgin Mary, which was finished around 1300. St. David's shrine is on the north choir aisle, where in the old days of pilgrimage there was a canopy with painted panels of Saints David, Patrick, and Dennis. The relics of St. David, believed to include some of his bones, are kept in a small casket at the original pilgrim recess, immediately in back of the altar wall.

St. David's monastic work, of tremendous influence in Wales, was in the old Celtic Christian Church, whose rituals and ways were quite different from those of Rome. The Celtic Church at St. David's did not come under the control of Canterbury and Rome until the twelfth century. With the sun breaking through the clouds and great streams of light seen upon the stone of the cathedral and the nearby ruins of the Bishop's Palace, the church catches a certain magical quality. Old St. David's retains the spirit of the esoteric and the Celtic, just as other parts of Wales reflect a certain uniqueness of religious spirit.

The Bishops' Palace is across the brook from the cathedral. The remaining fourteenth-century arches are exceptionally attractive and exude a spirit of enchantment. From the old esoteric standpoint, an arch is built above the earth's surface as a continuation of what is below, making a complete circle, incorporating within it the four elements of earth, water, fire, and air. The gifted New England psychic, Louisa M. Poole, was immediately drawn to the area of the Bishops' Palace upon arriving at St. David's. There she felt a great aliveness, with every little nook and corner needing further investigation as she felt overwhelming vibrations. An old world temple must have stood there earlier, and the ancient worship of the Mother Goddess is still felt there today.

John Wesley's thirty-four preaching tours in Wales made a difference, too, for his sympathy with the old religion, his use of the love feast, and his cooperation with the Welsh revivalist and religious communitarian Howell Harris have given a distinctive quality to the country's spiritual environment. The magic and mystery of the old ways and beliefs, the touch of both Wesleyans and "modern Druids," blend well with the Celtic faith of St. David, rightly called the Patron Saint of Wales.

Tips for Travelers

From London, trains run from Paddington Station to Cardiff, Wales, and coach service runs from there to other points.

Brecon is a lovely center for the visitor to southern Wales. Near the lush Brecon Beacon National Park, the old town itself is rich in historic associations and lore. The ancient cathedral is filled with strong spiritual vibrations. Brecon is about 200 miles round trip by car or coach from St. David's. The roads are good, and A 40 goes through a very attractive countryside. Passing through Carmarthen, take A 487 to the furthest tip of Wales at St. David's. Attractive places to stay are available near the sea in the area of Newgale and at St. David's.

About a mile out of Brecon, east of town, is Bishop's Meadow Motel, a plain and modest place of lodging with good food and the proverbial electric tea kettle with coffee, tea, and cocoa supplied.

HEREFORD

On the River Wye a few miles east of the Welsh border is the fascinating Hereford Cathedral. The town itself, built largely along the left bank, is very old and has been a seat of a bishop since 672. While only a few remnants of the once-turreted fortress are on the Castle Green, a number of fine half-timbered buildings can be seen.

The great Cathedral of Our Lady and St. Ethelbert is beautifully situated in a spacious close only a short distance from the Wye. Ethelbert, not to be confused with the earlier king with the same name in Kent, was an exemplary young prince of East Anglia who had come to the Mercian king's palace in 792 seeking the daughter's hand. There he was murdered by the king's men. The scandal aroused such indignation among the people that Ethelbert was soon considered a martyr. While his body was buried at Marden, Ethelbert's spirit appeared numerous times demanding burial at Hereford, which was done. Miraculous happenings began to take place on the site of the grave and chapel. In time the cathedral was built and dedicated to the Virgin Mary and St. Ethelbert.

It was in the early tenth century that the cathedral was rebuilt upon the older foundation, under the direction of Bishop Aethelstan, master builder and scholar. A warm and friendly feeling surrounds this beautiful edifice, adorned with art works and shrines. The shrine of St. Thomas Cantilupe, Bishop of Hereford from 1275 to 1282, attracted pilgrims in great numbers in the past and was widely known for miraculous cures. The shrine is a hallowed place still, the 700th anniversary of the good bishop's transition being celebrated with a festival of music and worship. The shrine is in the north transept.

Certain treasures should not be missed by today's traveler to Hereford. The Baptismal Font, which is as old as the cathedral, should be seen. It dates from Norman times and is near the main entry on the south aisle of the nave. Around the beautiful bowl are the sculpted figures of the twelve apostles. Another must is the great medieval Map of the World, made on vellum and drawn by Richard of Haldingham about 1290. Jerusalem is shown in the center, with the earth enclosed within the circle of the ocean. The map was intended to give information about geography, history, religion, and folklore, all pictured within a circle. One should secure from the cathedral shop a simple guide of this World Map and then go to see it on the north choir aisle.

Continue along this aisle to the exquisite Lady Chapel, built early in the thirteenth century. The beautiful reredos of more recent times depicts scenes from Mary's life.

Those who are interested in experiencing strong spiritual energies may wish to pause a few minutes in quiet in the south transept along the east wall, which is the oldest part of the cathedral. I found strong vibrations here, as did two others in our group.

One of the most exciting features of Hereford is the famous Chained Library, now housed in its old place, the upper transept room, which is reached from the north choir aisle by a narrow circular stone stairway. There are 1,500 chained books in this most fascinating of libraries, and of this number 227 are manuscript works, many going back a thousand years. Probably the oldest is the volume containing the Anglo-Saxon Gospels, dated A.D. 800. These books have a strong spiritual aura of saints and scholars of centuries past, and the entire library is probably the best example of its kind in the world.

The area surrounding Hereford has much to see. To the east are the lovely Malvern Hills, filled with history and legend and known for curative springs and holy wells. To both the north and west of Hereford are many unspoiled villages with black and white timbered buildings, apple orchards, and the well-known red and white faced Hereford cattle grazing on the hills. On a hill in this quiet and unspoiled section between Hereford and the Welsh border Alfred Watkins (1855–1935) received a visionary experience—the sight of a vast web of lines that seemed to come out of antiquity linking time-honored holy places. Old stones, crosses, church sites, holy wells, and spirit-filled trees appeared in an amazing alignment, the lines, sometimes called ley lines, running as great currents of vitality and telluric energy. Mystics of earlier times had similar experiences, referring to the fairy paths and the tracks of the angels. Watkins felt these lines had religious significance, and many scholars with the mystical bent have felt, too, that the clues to understanding our relation to the spiritual powers and Mother Earth can be seen in these unusual blendings. Watkins saw an especially vivid line connecting Hereford, Monmouth, and Brecon, where the ancient tracks are deep in the soil as if to show pilgrims the way to holy places. What is sometimes called the art or science of geomancy today may differ little from Biblical counsel such as the Proverb, "remove not the ancient landmarks which thy fathers have set," and the words from the Prophet Jeremiah, "See, and ask for the old paths, where is the good way, and walk therein, and ye shall find rest for your souls."[4]

Many romantic old scenes grace the way south of Hereford along the Wye. About thirty miles away is Tintern Abbey, where the picturesque ruins of the old thirteenth-century Cistercian buildings evoke a spirit of quiet reflection. Just a few miles above the abbey, William Wordsworth (1770–1850) composed some of his most memorable lines describing:

[4]Prov. 22:28, and Jer. 6:16

"the joy of elevated thoughts," and that "sense sublime
Of something far more deeply interfused . . ."[5]

Tips for Travelers

The border country of England and Wales is called the Marches. It is an area of hills and streams, quiet old towns, ruined castles, and many holy places. A well-planned day's trip by car from Stratford-upon-Avon could include Hereford, the Malvern Hills, and the historic Cathedral at Worcester. If Brecon (Wales) is one's center, a good day's trip could include Hereford and the Black Mountains.

For one staying in Hereford, the Green Dragon Hotel on Broad Street near the cathedral has a good reputation.

CANTERBURY

In the southeastern corner of England, on the River Stour within the ancient kingdom of Kent, is historic Canterbury. This picturesque city was known in Roman times as Durovernum. The name later changed to Cantwarabyrig, which means "borough of the men of Kent."

A Benedictine monastery had been founded there by the missionary Saint Augustine (not to be confused with the earlier noted theologian of the same name), who arrived with a group of monks in 597. A church was erected on the site of a ruined Roman structure, in the area where the old gods were worshiped. In time this became the cathedral, and Augustine is considered the first Archbishop of Canterbury.

King Ethelbert, a thoughtful and tolerant ruler of Kent, gave Augustine permission to preach the Gospel. Queen Bertha,

---

[5] William Wordsworth, "Lines composed a few miles above Tintern Abbey," in *The Book of Classic English Poetry,* ed. Edwin Markham (New York: Wm. H. Wise & Co., 1934), p. 1388.

who was of French background, was already a Christian. Later, when Ethelbert became a Christian, he insisted that the country be free in religious practice, that one become a Christian only on a voluntary basis, and that non-Christians be allowed to practice the old religions. It is strange that this enlightened monarch was never canonized, and yet his character and tolerance lend an authentic sanctity to the ground upon which he stood. Canterbury had had an earlier church. The Venerable Bede records that Queen Bertha worshiped in a little church on the east side of the town dedicated to St. Martin, which was built when the Romans were there.

In 1070 the great perpendicular cathedral was begun, and four centuries later Bell Harry, the famous tower, was erected. Canterbury, as the episcopal seat of the primate of the Church of England and a town of rich history, attracts travelers of many backgrounds. It has long been a place of pilgrimage, although its special note in this regard followed the martyrdom of Archbishop Thomas à Becket, who was murdered by the men of King Henry II on 29 December 1170. While Becket had earlier been a favorite of the king, he put his loyalty to God first after becoming archbishop. Henry's complaint against Becket was probably misunderstood by his henchmen when they committed their crime. Almost at once Thomas Becket was called a Christian martyr, and people from all over Britain and the continent journeyed as pilgrims to Canterbury. Miracles occurred at the place of the martyrdom and, as G. K. Chesterton used to comment, "there broke forth an epidemic of healing." The king himself went in penitence, and Louis VII of France went to ask for and to receive healing for his sick son. Miracles continued at Becket's shrine even after it was demolished by Henry VIII in 1538.

For more than three centuries pilgrimages were made to Canterbury, where great numbers received blessing and healing. Many others made the journey a merrymaking holiday, which has its value, too. Geoffrey Chaucer describes the vast variety of men and women on these pilgrimages, especially portraying some of the lighter aspects, in his *Canterbury Tales*, which first appeared about 1387. The pious and the not-so-pious, old and young, adventurers and vacationers, from countryside, village, and city

> pilgrims were they all
> That toward Canterbury town would ride.[6]

A reading from a modern English version of the tales adds interest to one's visit to Canterbury.

Scholars interested in geomancy believe that Canterbury, like some of the other great cathedrals and churches built over the ruins of Roman temples, is actually on the site of ancient megalithic circles. The very stones carry the right spiritual vibrations, and when incorporated into the foundations and walls of the newer structure they help to transmit the telluric energies of Mother Earth as well as the celestial influences. One can reasonably believe that some of the early Benedictines were well-acquainted with these perennial esoteric ideas and practices.

The traveler of today might well approach the cathedral through the fourteenth-century West Gate and then turn down Mercery Lane for the last few hundred exciting steps toward the entry. If arriving by train from London, one can take Castle Street to Mercery Lane. Mercery Lane is the historic pilgrims' way. After looking at the statues of Queen Bertha, Queen Elizabeth I, and the others, the traveler will enter a place of haunting beauty. The site of Becket's martyrdom is in the northwest transept, and Trinity Chapel, in back of the main altar, is where his shrine stood. The shrine of St. Dunstan, the great theologian and scholar, formerly of Glastonbury and later Archbishop of Canterbury, drew many pilgrims seeking intercessory prayers, especially for healing. This was probably between the choir and the main altar in the old days.

---

[6] Geoffrey Chaucer, *Canterbury Tales*, Modern English Edition (Garden City, N.Y.: Garden City Publishing Co., 1934), p. 2.

The oldest part of the cathedral is the spacious crypt, dedicated to the Virgin and entered from the southwest transept. A special chapel is for the French Protestants, who have worshiped here since 1563. In the crypt is the holy well, from which the waters have been used for curative purposes. How fortunate to arrive in Canterbury some sunny afternoon and sit on the grass to hear the tones of the majestic organ being played from the mighty console inside.

A short pleasant walk takes the visitor from the cathedral to the ruins of St. Augustine's Abbey. The twentieth-century excavations reveal interesting aspects of its Christian history, but there seems much more to be revealed. The number of early altars honoring Mary could well indicate a close relation to the pre-Christian worship of the Mother Goddess on this same sacred ground.

This colorful old city of Canterbury has an endless line of associations. It has been variously pictured according to the teller's own inward bent. Charles Dickens gives his description in *David Copperfield,* for David went to school there. It was Uriah Heep's home, too. Canterbury is a winsome town, with its black and white timbered houses and flower boxes protruding from under the windows, along the banks of the narrow Stour. The surrounding countryside has a variety of charms and is especially characterized by the many conical-shaped *oasthouses,* where hops dry out above a fire. The scene is completed by the apple orchards, the thatched roofed cottages and their lovely gardens, pleasant pastures, marsh lands, and deep forests.

Tips for Travelers

Frequent train service runs from London's Victoria Station to Canterbury, making an ideal one-day round trip excursion, with sufficient time to see the cathedral, the abbey ruins, and some of the fascinating old streets. The trip is sixty-two miles by car, and it is another eighteen miles to Dover, with its famed castle, its storied white cliffs, and the harbor where the ferries depart for Calais, Ostende, and the continent. Road A2 from London via Rochester and Canterbury to Dover follows the historic route of the Roman Watling Street, the great road of the Roman Empire days. The route has associations with King Arthur, with pilgrims and crusaders, and with characters from Shakespeare and Dickens.

NORTHERN FRANCE

CHARTRES

Many consider the Cathedral of Our Lady at Chartres the most magnificent edifice of Christendom, and many, too, feel it is a supernatural outgrowth of one of Mother Earth's most universal and perennial holy places. Some sixty miles southwest of Paris, the cathedral has spires that can be seen for miles across the fertile fields of Beauce. For centuries pilgrims have walked the ancient roads that lead to Chartres, and in the spring especially thousands of students still make the pilgrimage on foot from Notre Dame in Paris to this majestic and mysterious building which has long been recognized as "the flower and the glory of holy Europe."

Travelers who appreciate Gothic architecture at its grandest and who are entranced by the exquisite colors of medieval stained glass and statuary of an ageless vitality adore Chartres. The great towers, representatives of the Old and New Testaments of the Bible, loom above the glorious facade, peopled with prophets and apostles. Great portals in the towers portray events in the lives of Christ and the Virgin, and the towers are awe-inspiring even to the nominally religious. The transept entrances, when viewed in conjunction with the mighty Gothic buttresses, provide a solid strength that blends with an aura of spiritual power in the stone-carved faces and forms of Melchisedek and the other great ones in the encompassing cloud of witnesses.

Chartres as a town, with its narrow medieval streets, is itself a charming place. Every block is permeated with a feeling of nearness to the great cathedral. One may be entranced a long while with the cathedral's exterior beauty, but one experiences the fullness of the magic upon entering the portals. The nave, with its wonderful vaulted ceiling, the great pillars and many chapels, the high altar, and the incomparable window of the Queen of Heaven, is a part of the beauty that is beheld. The great rose window in the west lifts the spiritual seeker into a veritable paradise as the sun's rays shine through in the late afternoon. The transept window that King Louis IX gave in obedient and whole-hearted tribute to the Virgin is rich in color and design. During World War II these precious medieval windows, the formulas for which are unknown today, were dismantled and placed carefully under the earth for protection. They were put back in their places after the hostilities.

This supreme structure, begun in 1195, stands over the ancient holy ground where the former Christian Churches from the third century had stood. It represents the work of the finest artists, stonemasons, and glaziers, of architectural giants like the Abbe Suger, and the cooperative devotion and labor of peasants and princes alike, all in adoration of the Virgin Mary. St. Louis himself, the greatest and noblest of all French kings, harnessed himself to the huge stones and helped pull them to their proper places. The building of this cathedral was a true labor of love and devotion, and the devout believe that it was the Virgin herself who really planned and directed the work.

Many mysteries are connected with Chartres. Early pagan cults, including the Druids, worshiped the Mother Goddess on this ground from time immemorial. The holy well is used for ritual healing, and the sacred mound is where ancient worship took place and over which the cathedral was erected. According to old mystical traditions, a special telluric current comes to a head on this mound. In the old days pilgrims went to do homage to Our Lady of Under-the-Earth, a Black Madonna with Child, which was a statue dating to pre-Christian times and believed to be carved by the Druids and blackened by age. The statue was kept as a holy relic in the crypt of the cathedral until the crypt was destroyed in the sixteenth century. Tradition has it that a prophetic angel announced to the Druidic priests that a Virgin would give birth to a Divine Son. The sculptor who did the Nativity scene over the royal entrance used for his model this ancient and revered Black Virgin from the crypt.

Some Chartres mysteries are of geomancy, believed to be an ancient science known to the pyramid builders and to St. Bernard of Clairvaux and the Knights Templars, where the human habitats and activities are brought into harmony with the invisible spiritual world. The French scholar Louis Charpentier contends that Chartres and certain other cathedrals were constructed along these esoteric lines involving geomancy, alchemy, and special forms of occult knowledge. It is interesting to note, for instance, that on June 21, the summer solstice, a ray of sun at midday precisely strikes a special rectangular flagstone, set aslant to the others. Fascinating data, too, support the idea that the secret dimensions of Solomon's Temple contained in the Ark of the Covenant apply to Chartres. Charpentier and others feel that the cathedral was built to serve as an instrument to store and release healing energy for the benefit of the locality, especially the pilgrims.

A maze, constructed of blue and white stone and about forty feet in diameter, is a part of the floor just beneath the beautiful twelve-fold west rose window. The maze and the window conform exactly in size, which could be symbolic of the celestial labyrinth touching that of the earth.

The old mystics and the new esotericists make much of these things, and often meaningful insights are caught when one meditates on such themes. The spiritually sensitive traveler will find many unusual mysteries at Chartres.

Henry Adams, in his classic book *Mont-Saint Michel and Chartres,* tells how the Cathedral of Chartres is a continuing witness to the passionate worship of Mary and how this worship elevated the feminine aspect of Deity. Tradition holds that the master glazier, the master carpenter, the master builders, and others received their guidance and directions from celestial agents, and perhaps directly from Mary, the revered Seat of Wisdom.

Pilgrims come to Chartres today, as in the past, out of their ardent love for Mary. In the Middle Ages great numbers of the sick were taken into the crypt where they could be especially close to Mother Earth and the Madonna and Child statue and where they could use the curative waters from the well. Healing abounded: paralytics were almost always made well and the wounded cured. In later centuries many would go to the main altar for healing or would pray in one of the many chapels surrounding the great nave. Some have always come to be close to the relics, especially to be near the tunic, believed by many to have been the Virgin's. The healing power continues in evidence in every generation. Many come to Chartres to simply admire the superb beauty of the place, but the beauty in its greatest dimension is only seen when the individual's spirit feels a certain rapport with that of the Queen of Heaven. The rapport is a spiritual experience of great intensity.

On one of my several visits to Chartres, seven thousand French school children had come on pilgrimage that day. Their unusual orderliness and reverence belied their youthfulness; they seemed to blend with the very purpose of the holy place, as their voices were lifted in songs of praise to Mary and her Son. Miracles still occur at Chartres, not only in the quietness and inspired hearts of those seven thousand children, but in the lives of all who come and find healing, peace, and new directions for life. A pilgrimage to Chartres is in essence a return to God, a restoring of harmony of spirit and mind and body. It is a recovery of a lost paradise, a coming home again, a returning to a place where the cooperative and transforming spiritual influences make for inner peace and renewal.

Tips for Travelers

Chartres may be reached from Paris by either rail or road, with several alternatives for the latter. A number of travel companies in Paris offer one-day guided tours by motor coach to the famous cathedral. Some include a visit to the lovely moated chateau at Maintenon, and others stop at the small and distinctive Chateau D'Anet.

While pilgrims are always visiting Chartres, the annual pilgrimage of students walking from Paris takes place at Whitsuntide. The town has some good small hotels and inns.

AMIENS

Whoever takes the boat train from London to Paris, crossing the channel between Dover and Calais and continuing by rail through the fields of Picardy, will see the skyline of Amiens with its greatest monument, the massive cathedral, dominating the scene. Yet the power of this place can never be felt until one takes the time and effort to visit the historic Cathedral of Our Lady.

The city itself, unlike Chartres, does not seem conducive to the cathedral's vibrations. A preoccupation with commerce and a frequency of wars make the area alien to a breakthrough of spiritual beauty, but the cathedral in its overwhelming majesty gives a vital witness to those with eyes to see and minds and hearts to fathom. In the early fourth century, St. Fermin, known as the confessor, had gone to northern France with the Gospel and had built a little chapel dedicated to the Virgin Mary. Fermin suffered martyrdom there, and in the subsequent years peasants found many blessings of healing and other miracles through the spirit of the holy man.

The present cathedral, built on the site of the former buildings, was begun about 1220 and was completed within a half century. It is the largest Gothic cathedral in France, is pure in design and style, and has been described as "clear of Romanesque tradition and of Arab taint." The divine message of its fabric is expressed with a perfection, serenity, and strength seldom equaled. It is "the Bible in stone," as John Ruskin, the great English art critic and moral essayist, has written. Christianity has never been pictured in stone with such vision, artistry, and perfection, as at Amiens.

Between the center doors at the cathedral's front is Christ giving His blessing, and on either side are the apostles and the prophets. Above the doors Christ is seen enthroned, with St. Michael weighing the souls of the departed, while the north portals are devoted to the life of St. Fermin and "the apostles of Amiens," surrounded by the local saints, both female and male. As with almost all Gothic cathedrals, the south portals depict scenes from the life and continuing intercession of the Virgin Mary. One of the greatest joys of a visit to Amiens is to enter at the south transept, where the incomparable Smiling Madonna is holding the Christ Child.

Entering Amiens for the first time is a memorable experience, for one is suddenly transported into another world. The nave is magnificent in its massiveness: it is very wide and measures 138 feet from the stone floor to its vaulted ceiling. It is warmly inviting with friendly vibrations, inspiring even the casual visitor and utterly enthralling the sensitive pilgrim. One cannot doubt that one stands on holy ground.

The medieval builders, with esoteric knowledge and spiritual vision, designed the nave to lead the eye in a continuing and rising movement, evoking aspirations for Heaven and adoration of God. The many side-chapels, the perfection of the statuary, the magnetism of the symbols such as the scallop shell, the crown of twelve stars, the rose, all reflecting devotion to the Great Mother, and the fantastic carvings of peasants and fairies, saints and angels, are among the facets of attraction.

Between the choir and the high altar is a maze forty-two feet in diameter on the floor, dating from the thirteenth century and restored in the nineteenth century. Such a maze suggests the labyrinthine ways a soul must go in the spiritual journey of salvation.

The choir area is one of the glories of the cathedral. John

Ruskin said that in the basilicas of northern Europe the choir area is the one distinctive part where the Divine Presence is believed to be constant. Done in about 1522, 3,650 figures are in carved oak at the choirstalls, and these represent 400 scenes from the Bible. They constitute one of the most complete carved portrayals of Scripture in Europe and certainly one of the most exquisitely rendered anywhere.

The traveler who wants to see and appreciate the French cathedrals will find something of unique delight in each. Nowhere in the world is there such an array of magnificent edifices within such a compact area as in France. Henry Adams once said that the closest thing to heaven on earth is to be driving through the French countryside on the way to a Gothic cathedral.

While a visit to any of these holy places can be a joy, surely none would surpass Chartres and Amiens.

Tips for Travelers

Take the train to Amiens from the Gare du Nord in Paris. If driving, one has several possibilities, including a day's trip that could also include Saint-Denis and the famed chateau at Chantilly, or a visit to the cathedral at Beauvais.

While considerable time is needed to see the marvels of the cathedral, Amiens has other sights, too. The Museum of Picardy contains very valuable art works, both medieval and modern.

PARIS

In Victor Hugo's classic novel, *The Hunchback of Notre Dame*, Paris is described as consisting of three parts: the Cité, which is the ancient island in the middle of the River Seine, the side known as the Left Bank, and the Right Bank. A number of places have been so long associated with religious worship in these three historic areas that they could be justly looked upon as holy ground. The River Seine has ancient links with pre-Christian centers of worship. The name Seine is believed to be derived from the Latin name Sequana, who was a goddess identified with healing waters. In antiquity a shrine to her stood at the headwaters of the Seine near present-day Dijon, and at various places along the banks of that celebrated river worship was conducted by devotees of the old religions. No doubt the goddess' presence was felt on the Ile de la Cité long before the coming of Christianity. In Roman times, after the great matriarchal age, a temple to Jupiter stood where the Cathedral of Notre Dame now stands. As early as the third century, people practiced Christian worship on this island, which looks like a great ship in the river. The present magnificent cathedral, dedicated to the Virgin Mary, was begun in 1163 under the direction of Bishop Maurice de Sully.

The Gothic grandeur of Notre Dame gives Paris its center of balance and beauty, and the spiritual emanations from this most famous of cathedrals reflect a light that has endured even through most dismal times. Whoever goes to Paris sees Notre Dame, and yet this popularity does not really diminish its spiritual power—a power felt by the sensitive pilgrim. The majesty of the exterior, caught in the familiar picture of this most historic landmark of Paris, is known to people all over the world. It is an exciting experience to climb to the towers, greeting the statuary saints and gargoyles on the balustrades, hearing Quasimodo ringing the great bells, and viewing all of Paris in its panoramic delights.

Visitors should enter Notre Dame from the front, noting the likeness of the Great Mother at the portal and the array of apostles and saints. One also sees St. Denis carrying his severed head in his hand. Around A.D. 258 Denis was beheaded at Montmartre, the hill of the martyrs on the far Right Bank, and legend says he walked to the site of the Basilica of St. Denis carrying his head.

Once inside Notre Dame, one is transported into another

world. The three thirteenth-century rose windows retain the original glass and are among the finest in existence. The very architecture of such a Gothic cathedral is overwhelmingly impressive. As Francois Chateaubriand (1768–1848) wrote: "These carved-stone vaults, these ceilings which seem so much like foliage, these columns and pilasters which support the walls, and, like broken tree trunks, are suddenly ended. . . . the shadowness of the sanctuary, obscure recesses, secret passages and crypts—all combine to make one experience a religious awe, mystery, and divinity."[1]

The old vitality has not been lost at Notre Dame. In one of my early visits to the cathedral I sat awhile in a quiet corner, and as I looked toward a small side chapel where Holy Communion was being given an elderly woman, I was struck by the appearance of the priest, his face aglow, his aura ever so bright. In that strange telepathic sense I knew the entranced priest was experiencing the joy of being encompassed by "the angels and the archangels, and all the company of heaven."

Tradition holds that relics of the True Cross and the Crown of Thorns were brought to the Cité in early times and were kept in or near the cathedral. Sainte-Chapelle, a perfect gem of Gothic architecture, was built a short distance from Notre Dame by King Louis IX (1214–1270), the sainted monarch and devotee of the Virgin Mary. The expressed purpose of this royal chapel was to be a depository for the sacred relics of Christ, fragments of the Cross and the Crown. The chapel, really two chapels with one for the royal family directly above the other for the servants, gives an impression of considerable height. The upper one is 118 feet long, fifty-six feet wide, and 138 feet high. The stained glass windows are of exquisite beauty, glistening and radiant. They tell the legend of the cross and of the removal of the relics, and they depict scenes from the Bible and the lives of the apostles and the martyrs.

[1] Marcel Belvianes, *French Cathedrals* (Novara, Italy: The Uffici Press, n.d.), p. 4.

St. Louis's role as a church builder is widely known and respected, as is his exemplary religious life, his championing civil liberties, and his wise counsel to his son on the moral responsibilities of a monarch. The remarkable biography *The Life of St. Louis* (Hague translation) by his friend John of Joinville is one of the most inspiring works of the thirteenth century, and makes most fascinating reading in today's translations. Since St. Louis's departure many healings have been ascribed to his intercession, and his spirit has manifested itself in highly evidential ways, even in very recent times.

While many places of unusual spiritual aura can be found in today's Paris, three distinctive sites on the Left Bank could be especially considered. St. Germain-des-Prés, on the long and picturesque boulevard of that name, is generally believed to be the oldest standing church in Paris. It is Romanesque in its basic style and has massive flying buttresses, among the earliest in France. A church was founded on this site as part of a Benedictine Abbey by Childebert I in the sixth century, and the good and humane Saint Germanus, Bishop of Paris, who died in 576, is honored here. His bones are buried under the church. The present structure, begun in the eleventh century, has continued as a center of spiritual influence through the centuries.

The immediate area of Place St. Sulpice has a number of reminders of great mystics, and no doubt at certain spots of the earth there holy experiences have taken place and still cause inspired feelings. A statue of the beloved Francois Fénelon (1651–1715), the great mystic and archbishop of Cambrai whose writings on Christian perfection and love are universally read, should quicken a seeker's interest in both Fénelon and Madame Guyon. Madame Guyon (1648–1717) was a friend of Fénelon and an amazing Christian saint, seer, and writer. Their friendship gave rise to a spirituality embracing and blessing both Protestants and Catholics. Both were cruelly persecuted— Madame Guyon was charged with heresy and imprisoned several years in the Bastille. Their strength and serenity, arising out of their acquaintance with an eternal world, have inspired subsequent generations, and both are still effectively invoked for intercession by the mystically inclined. One can find many associations with them in Paris, Versailles, and other places in France. Jean Marie de la Mothe Guyon remained in hiding for some months in a small apartment in the Faubourg St. Antoine, just east of the Place de la Bastille. At one time Fénelon lived at 3 rue St. Louis-en-L'lie, on the little island in the Seine, just beyond the Cité.

St. Sulpice Church has its own unique association with mysticism, too, and especially with a famous, simple, and effective method of meditation. This imposing classical structure, with its tower 240 feet high and its spacious interior 360 feet long, was begun in 1646 on the site of an older church. Lovely chapels encircle the church within, and one chapel has paintings by Ferdinand Delacroix. Late in the seventeenth century a little group of devout laypersons and priests met regularly for prayer and simple meditation. They developed what is called the Sulpician Method of Meditation, which consists of focusing on three consecutive ideas: Christ in my eyes, Christ in my heart, and Christ in my hands. This method of attaining an increasing spiritual consciousness is still used by many people today.

Another place of spiritual power on the Left Bank is at 140 rue du Bac, an ancient street that crosses Boulevard St. Germain. It is the Seminary of the Daughters of Charity, and there in 1830 the twenty-three-year-old Catherine Labouré had a series of visions of the Virgin Mary. The first apparition appeared on the night of the feast day of St. Vincent de Paul and took place in the chapel, where the Virgin conversed with Catherine for more than two hours. In subsequent appearances Catherine was instructed by Mary to have a medal made, to be worn by people who especially seek the Great Mother's blessing. The letter "M" is on the medal, with two hearts, one encircled by a crown of thorns, the other pierced with a sword. Around the monogram are twelve stars that refer to the New Testament description in the twelfth chapter of the Book of Revelation of the Great Woman upon whose head is a crown of twelve stars of the zodiac. St. Catherine Labouré died in 1876. When the vault was opened a half century later, her body was absolutely intact and was placed under the Altar of the Apparitions. The miraculous medal has been used by millions of people. Many have attested to special blessings, and the ground where the chapel stands on rue du Bac has been the scene of healings through the years.

The massive group of buildings along the rue des Ecoles on the Left Bank is part of one of the oldest and greatest universities in the world, the University of Paris. The historic center of the University is the Sorbonne, the famous school of theology founded in 1253 by Robert de Sorbon, chaplain to St. Louis. Here major theologians of the centuries have helped mold religious thought. Near the Sorbonne is the Museum of Cluny, the buildings dating to the fifteenth century and containing treasured relics of the Middle Ages and art works of unusual religious significance.

Any serious visitor to Paris will want to spend some time in the Louvre, one of the largest palaces in the world that houses one of the greatest collections of art treasures in existence. The Louvre has so much to see that it has been said "no one has ever seen the Louvre," for no one has really seen more than parts of it. On the rue de Rivoli, extending to the Right Bank of the Seine, the vast buildings dating from 1204 have been enlarged over the centuries by the kings and governments. The Greek and Roman collections include the famous Venus de Milo, The Winged Victory, and great works of sculpture from before the time of Christ. The Louvre also has the antiquities of Sumerian, Egyptian, and other civilizations and religious traditions, and great paintings by the major artists of our heritage. Leonardo da Vinci's Mona Lisa, superb religious masterpieces by Fra Angelico and Botticelli, the spectacular Rubens room, and wonderful works by Titian, Raphael, and Rembrandt are but the beginning of the galleries of delight to be seen in the Louvre. Copies and reproductions can be purchased in an excellent shop.

On the rue de Rivoli, just west of the rue du L[...] be seen the Coligny Monument, which is outside the[...] Protestant Reformed Church of the Oratoire. Nea[...] miral Gaspard de Coligny (1517–1572), the Hugu[...] and champion of religious freedom, was murdered during the St. Bartholomew Day massacre. I have paused there many times to quietly reflect on the New Testament words beneath the statue: "He endured as seeing Him who is invisible."

If one continues eastward on the rue de Rivoli, beyond the Louvre a tall tower will soon loom on the horizon. It is St. Jacques Tower, all that remains of the Church of St. Jacque de la Boucherie. In the past the devout assembled at the tower before setting out on pilgrimage for Orleans and the Shrine of St James the Apostle in Spain. Near the tower, too, in hidden chambers, the alchemists and practitioners of the old religion would gather in secret.

Varied and rich is the history of Paris, and from its patron St. Genevieve to Abelard and St. Louis, to Brother Lawrence and St. Vincent de Paul, Fénelon and Jean Marie Guyon and Catherine Labouré, the line of devotion and love has kept aflame, even amid changing tides of war and revolution, bigotry and persecution. Holy ground remains and with it remains a continuing spirit, humane and inspiring.

Tips for Travelers

No way of seeing Paris is better than by foot. Although public transportation is very good, some of the most fascinating surprises are found while walking along little side streets. Nor is there any substitute for a stroll along one of the main boulevards or avenues or beside the Seine. In choosing a hotel visitors should find one in an area of greatest interest—for the pilgrim this means in the central and older parts of Paris. On the Right Bank the Hotel de France et Choisseul, 239–241 rue St. Honore, is excellently located. Near the Place Vendome and only a block from the rue de Rivoli, this eighteenth-century uilding, refurbished for today's traveler, has a lovely court and some reminders of a past age. It is within a few minutes walk from the Louvre, the opera, the Tuileries Gardens, and the Place de la Concorde. Many pleasant and often more reasonably priced small hotels and pensions are on the Left Bank.

Good day excursions by coach with guide are available to many places of interest, including to the Palace and Gardens of Versailles, to Fontainebleau, to the Cathedrals at Chartres, Reims, Amiens, and Rouen, or to the Shrine of St. Teresa the Little Flower at Lisieux. Some of the cathedral tours include a stop at one of the chateaux. The hotel concierge can usually offer assistance in suggesting a train schedule for an all-day visit to one of the cathedrals or to the chateau country.

TEUTONIC LANDS

A vast area in Germany, stretching more than a hundred miles from Karlsruhe to Basle and from Freiburg eastward for more than fifty miles, has long been known as the Black Forest. With its mountain ridges and valleys, curative springs and streams, fairy-story villages and deep dark woods, it is a land of enchantment, replete with timeless legends and folk traditions.

Sibyls, seers, and saints have dwelt in these historic areas. Practitioners of the old religion and evangels of the new have mingled in the matchless beauty of the Black Forest. Old pilgrimage churches, monastic centers dedicated to the Virgin, and holy wells used for sacerdotal and healing purposes from earliest times abound. The woodland spirits and the fairy people described in tales from the Brothers Grimm, Jacob (1783–1863) and William (1786–1859), are not difficult for the sensitive to find. Such legendary personalities as Doctor Faustus, the alchemist and occultist, wandered often through the Black Forest, and the great Paracelsus acquired some of his vast knowledge of the esoteric on his travels through these enchanted woods.

Freiburg un Breisgau, on the southwestern edge of the great forest, is a lovely city. The *Minster* (or "Cathedral") of Our Lady, one of Germany's finest examples of classical Gothic architecture, was begun around 1200. The famous filigree spire, which is 377 feet high, is a much-loved landmark. The interior, with its fine old stained glass windows and the beautiful altarpiece of the Coronation of the Virgin by Hans Grien, and the

University Chapel, with its panels of the Nativity and the Adoration of the Magi by Hans Holbein the Younger, give the place a fairyland quality. On a market day, the colorful fruits and vegetables in the immediate front of the minster offer an attractive natural prelude to the feeling of a supernal dimension one feels upon entering the sanctuary.

In the southerly part of the Black Forest the hills rise rather steeply, reaching an elevation of 4,905 feet at the Feldberg, a few miles east of Freiburg.

The Titisee-Neustadt section is especially charming. While Titisee presents a beautiful mountain lake encompassed by many hostelries for both summer and winter visitors, one is never far from the unspoiled woods. The town of Neustadt is a very old one and in its simplicity retains an undeniable charm. The old minster church of St. James dates from the Middle Ages, and a short distance from there by foot one can come to clear sparkling streams flowing from the velvety woods through a little park of sheer magical influence. In the opposite direction from the church, another short walk to the south, is seen the ancient spring with its curative waters flowing through the town, with flower-decked banks on either side. An attractive wrought-iron sign points the way to the Kneipp spa. The latter is one of the many spas throughout the Black Forest that uses the Kneipp water method of healing. A nineteenth-century priest, Father Sebastian Kneipp (1821–1897), developed this well-known water cure, used to heal many types of illness. Kneipp believed the waters of Mother Earth held divinely given healing properties and that when used according to a certain form of hydrotherapy would produce good results.

Such healing waters were used by the peasants of former times for many types of curative blessings even as they are used today, with the encouragement of medical people and other therapists. They save men and women from the unnecessary costs, fright, and medications of hospitals.

St. Margen, also long associated as a climatic health place, is beautifully situated on a plateau within view of the Feldberg. An Augustinian monastery had been established here in the early twelfth century, and a Romanesque statue of the Virgin Mary took on special powers, becoming an object of veneration for pilgrims. Today's baroque tower of the rebuilt church may be seen for miles around. The interior of the building seems to contain an unbroken aura of spiritual power.

In the little villages of the woods stand many such churches, which have been centers for retreat and pilgrimage for hundreds of years. The spiritually sensitive person will become aware of the vibrations in certain old sanctuaries and in the adjoining cemeteries that are hidden in these magical valleys.

The forest cultus, which has certain universal implications, is an essential part of the old Germanic tradition. Woods and wooded meadows were sacred to the gods, and a great tree often stood for a deity. Jacob Grimm, the foremost authority on Teutonic mythology, held that the idea of Holy Wood is traced to the old religion, becoming in time a part of the Christian tradition where it is associated with the cross and the altar. In the forests the soul finds a nearness to both the greater deities and to the woodland spirits. In the Black Forest and other mysterious woods, the religious practice of carving figures in trees to represent the spirits has gone on from earliest times. When the very spirit in back of the life of the tree is recognized by a sensitive person, a sort of telepathic communication is established between the two. This kinship between human beings and the elementals of nature is important to the understanding of certain truths found in the old folklore and religions. The sacredness of the forest and especially of particular trees are a part of an ancient religious heritage that blends, perhaps providentially, with the biblical and cabalistic ideas of the Tree of Life.

Today's traveler who keeps a bit open to the supernormal will find the Black Forest exciting and enchanting. In this spirit, too, can be a feeling of peace and joy, as "the mountains and the hills break forth . . . into singing, and all the trees of the field . . . clap their hands."[1]

[1] Isaiah 55:12.

From the Frankfurt airport, coaches, trains, and private cars are available south to the Black Forest region. It is about three hours by rail or highway from Frankfurt to Freiburg, which is a good place for entering this picturesque area. Frequent coach service is available from Freiburg to the villages and towns of the southern Black Forest.

The Titisee-Neustadt area can be reached from Freiburg on Route 31. Neustadt makes a fine center for seeing the area. The Post-Adler Hotel, associated with the Romantik Inns, is a delightful place for lodging and food. It dates from the sixteenth century and has been operated by the same family for many years.

THE BAVARIAN ALPS

In one of the most scenic sections of Europe generally known as the Bavarian Alps, spiritual vibrations are strong in some distinctive places. Such notable religious centers as Ettal and Oberammergau are in the Ammergau range. A good base for seeing this great area is Garmisch-Partenkirchen, ideally situated near the foot of the Zugspitze. At more than 9,700 feet high, it is the highest mountain in Germany.

Atop the Zugspitze, which is accessible by cable car, is one of the grandest views of Europe. One can see the miles of mountain ranges with their great glaciers, the majestic Alps of Austria and Switzerland, and, on a clear day, one can see the distant Dolomites of northern Italy.

Garmisch, with its lovely chalets, the beautiful baroque church of St. Martin's, the rambling house so long the residence of the great composer Richard Strauss, the good hotels and shops, the enchanting vistas in all directions, and the easy access to trails into the woods and mountains, can be a center for visiting the nearby Austrian alpine villages and valleys as well as the

German Ammergau. The area has a fine railroad system with many trains going in all directions, and the station is within walking distance of the center of town. The Alte Kirche has been a place of worship since 1280, and only in recent years have remarkable fourteenth-century murals been uncovered. When one has walked through this older section of the town, passing a wayside shrine, one sees a quaint entry to this old church and can experience a feeling of entering another age. It is a good old church in which to reflect awhile, with an appealing simplicity in its interior.

Ettal Abbey is but ten or twelve miles from Garmisch. In the heart of the hills of the Ammergau, Ettal is a magnificent sight, the great baroque structure astonishingly spacious. This abbey of the Benedictine Order is equally beautiful inside, with its round polygonal sanctuary and the great dome with its lovely murals. The present structure is from the eighteenth century but, of course, is founded upon a much earlier edifice. Upon the altar is the exquisite little fourteenth-century statue of the Virgin Mary, an object of great veneration and believed to be endowed with miracle-working powers.

In the early 1300s Ludwig the Bavarian king was held captive in Italy, and he turned to God, vowing he would establish a monastery if he could return to his beloved home in the valley of the high hills of the Ammergau. Help came to Ludwig, and he built the abbey at Ettal "to the glory of God and the honour of our Lady." An old tradition says that one time while he was praying, he was visited by a monk who gave him a miraculous image of the Virgin and told him he would be given special aid. He took the statue, and while in a dense forest his horse suddenly stood still and struck the ground three times with his hoof. The king took this as a sign from heaven, and on that site the forest was cleared and the abbey built.

Pilgrims have come to Ettal for more than six hundred years, and Mary's healing power has been experienced by many who approach the shrine with faith and devotion. The abbey has faced some severe hardships and attacks from invading nonbelievers, and a number of times the precious statue has been secretly removed and hidden. Yet the spiritual powers remain, and the Great Mother's help to sincere seekers remains evident.

A short two or three miles north of Ettal is one of the most famous little towns of Europe, Oberammergau. It is a very attractive place, with charming painted houses depicting old legends and fairy stories, a fine parish church with a rococo altar, and many shops with carvings by the local woodcarvers. The renown of Oberammergau is because of the Passion Play, presented by the villagers every ten years and drawing thousands of people from all over the world. Generally about 100 performances are given during the summer months by 1,700 amateur players, drawn from the local community. This presentation of the Passion of the Lord Christ is one of the great dramatic and religious spectacles of Europe.

The origin of the play is indicative of a special spiritual aura surrounding the little town. A dreadful plague swept through many sections of Europe in 1632, and some folk believe the prayers of the faithful stopped the epidemic just before it reached Oberammergau. A grateful people vowed to enact the Gospel narrative every decade, and using a German text that has been revised several times through the years, generation after generation of devout folks from this little Bavarian town have given this much-admired Passion Play. The first presentation was in 1634, and it has been enacted every ten years since (excluding once during the World War), with a special showing for 1984, marking 350 years.

In these Ammergau Alps are several picturesque castles that have become among the best-known and most enchanting anywhere. They are associated with the nineteenth-century Bavarian monarch, dreamer, idealist, and builder, King Ludwig II. While elusive and eccentric, this noble king has been much maligned and misunderstood. But in more recent times an increasing number of people appreciate both his architectural genius and his high spiritual purposes. He was the friend and benefactor of Richard Wagner, the supreme music-drama composer of all times. Had it not been for Ludwig's insight, courage, and generosity, the world may not have had some of Wagner's most inspiring and meaningful music.

The old twelfth-century castle of Hohenschwangen had fallen into ruin when rebuilt by Maximilian II in 1832–36 and was refurbished with murals of Nordic myths by Ludwig II. It was here that Wagner visited Ludwig. Here, too, the king planned, directed, and watched the building of the nearby Neuschwanstein, the magnificent fairytale Castle, whose turrets seem to reach into another dimension on misty days. It is probably the most frequently pictured castle in the world. The interior is replete with handsome paintings of a mystical nature, from the apse of the throne-hall and its portrayal of Christ, the Virgin Mary, and St. John to other rooms with scenes from Wagner's *Parsifal, Tannhauser, Lohengrin,* and *Tristan und Isolde.* The ornate Linderhof Castle, also built by Ludwig, just a few miles from Ettal, is of a French design. The castle is a sort of miniature Versailles, with lovely gardens and fountains and an imaginatively created Venus Grotto for esoteric presentations of Wagner's operas.

The perennial Teutonic mythology still lives in the Bavarian Alps. The dreams of the great builder Ludwig and the genius of the amazing musician–mystic Wagner are evident, their spirits strongly permeating the area today. The minnesingers may still be heard in the wooded hills singing their praises of the mighty Brunhilda, and the swans, birds of Augury, remind us of the magical maidens ever inhabiting the sylvan scenes and secluded streams of Bavaria.

The old Teutonic troubadors would tell, and Wagner reechoes the theme anew, of a golden age of peace, which could have lasted always but was broken by the greed for gold which brought about the first wars. Monsters came and devoured the old giants and heroes, swallowing them whole, and the destruction meant the twilight of the old order. But a new world is born, and the new gods are really those old ones who had kept the faith and who had never succumbed to evil and violence. They never perished, and they are to renew the world in peace. Parsifal, Wagner is saying, heralds the new day in proclaiming redeeming love, exemplified in the highest and greatest of the perennial gods, Christ.

Tips for Travelers

Garmisch-Partenkirchen is an ideal center for seeing the area of the Bavarian Alps. From the Munich airport Garmisch is a little more than sixty miles southwest by road or rail.

The town has many fine inns. The Wittelsbach Hotel is excellent and well-run, with especially good food and fine service. Many of the rooms have balconies from which to view the Alps. The hotel office will book tours to see King Ludwig's Castles, or Oberammergau and Ettal, or the Zugspitze and other alpine wonders.

ULM

On the banks of the Danube River, less than a hundred miles east of its source in the Black Forest, rises the great cathedral tower of Ulm, the highest in the world. It is 520 feet tall, and, while designed in the late Middle Ages, it was not completed until 1890.

The cathedral is one of the largest and most majestic in Germany, and, as the Minster of Our Lady, the present structure was begun in the late fourteenth century. Long before this the ground was considered a holy place, and many devotees of Christ and Mary have been associated with it. Blessed Henry Suso (c. 1295–1366), one of the great mystics of Christianity whose classic writings still stir the hearts of many, lived in Ulm the last forty years of his priestly and prophetic life. There the saintly young Elsbeth Stagel, whom he had trained in the faith, appeared to Henry during the years after her early death, giving him counsel from the heavenly world. These experiences and those of his lifetime contact with the Virgin Mary are recorded in his remarkable autobiography and devotional writings. In Ulm, too, the old legends have it, Suso was feeling downcast one day as Christmas approached and was suddenly transported to a joyful mood when an angel came and danced with him. The angel, while dancing Suso around, inspired him with a merry spirit and, it is said, taught him the celestial words and the tune of what we now know as "Good Christian Men, Rejoice!", one of our best-loved Christmas carols.

Many local folk of faith from the medieval age as well as better-known saints are depicted in the statuary of the magnificent cathedral. The interior of the great edifice is filled with wonders. The exquisite choir stalls, made under the direction of Jörg Syrlin the Elder from 1469–74, have wood-carved busts of the ancient philosophers and poets from Pythagoras to Virgil, and of the great wise women such as the sibyls of Cumae and Phrygia. So remarkably done are these figures of the sibyls, so realistic and full of expression, that the woodcarving artist must have been attuned with their immortal spirits. I have never seen a finer appreciation of the various sibyls than at Ulm; the carvings are comparable with Michelangelo's fresco representations of them in the Sistine Chapel. The Cumean sibyl had prophesied the birth of Christ, and all of these great women are linked as the transmitters of both telluric energy and prophetic truth.

After the cathedral became Protestant, an imposing statue of the great reformer and theologian Martin Luther (1483–1546) was erected in the nave, as were likenesses of such German composers as Johann Sebastian Bach (1685–1750) and George Frederic Handel (1685–1759).

Away from the main altar is the little Besserer Chapel, dated 1414. In it are some very small stained and brightly colored glass windows showing scenes from the Bible. These little windows, among the most exquisite to be seen anywhere, were done by the master artist Hans Acker in 1431. Among the scenes, especially striking is that of Noah's ark, where the land-scape becomes a part of the interpretation. The wild clouds and the foam-covered waters help tell the story, as the dove returns with its twig to Noah. A lovely transparency of this scene is included in the official guidebook at Ulm Cathedral. On the other side of the altar is the Neithart Chapel, begun in 1444, after the donor's son was healed through the intercession of St. Valentine.

The city of Ulm itself is very interesting, and the streets in the old fisherman's quarters and the walks along the banks of the Danube are reminiscent of a still-lingering romanticism. But the cathedral is the central focus, and no pilgrim can see it or wander through the vast interior or climb up beyond the bells of the great tower, without feeling something of a supernal power.

Tips for Travelers

Ulm, which is on the Danube River, is a little more than an hour by rail from Stuttgart, less than two hours from Munich, and four hours from Frankfurt. It is four miles south of the main Highway 8, which runs between Munich and Stuttgart. Highway 311 connects Ulm with the Black Forest in the west. About forty-five miles directly east of Ulm is the Romantic Road.

Hotel Neutor-Hospiz is an attractive place to stay, with a spectacular circular stairway and lovely rooms. The hotel is but a short walk from the market plaza and the great cathedral.

ROTHENBURG ON THE TAUBER

From Fussen, in the Bavarian Alps, the old Romantic Road runs northward through peaceful valleys and a lovely countryside to the River Main. The Romans had traveled this way from the time of Christ, and the road is a veritable journey through history. The troubadours of Our Lady, the mastersingers and folk poets, the Teutonic knights and seekers of the Holy Grail, and pilgrims from many lands are all part of the ongoing story of the Romantic Road. The road has variety and charm all the way, passing the larger cities like Augsburg and Wurzburg as well as the many smaller towns—such medieval places as Donauworth, Nordlingen, Dinkelsbuhl, and Feuchtwangen.

One of the oldest and best-preserved towns to be crossed by the Romantic Road is walled Rothenburg, with its castles and ramparts, church towers and gabled houses, winding streets and flowing fountains. It is a treasure of medieval beauty on the banks of the River Tauber. First mentioned in the chronicles in 804 as Rotinbure, it appears as a town in 842. In 1108 it passed to the legendary Hohenstaufen family and by the end of that century had become a free imperial city. Rothenburg was a prosperous place of trade and commerce in the fourteenth and fifteenth centuries, then later settled into a long period of quiet, becoming in modern times the old and perennial gem sought by travelers for its medieval charm.

At the town's highest point loom the towers of St. Jacob's Church, a place of holiness and beauty that has attracted pilgrims through the centuries. The Gothic structure was built upon an older one, for statues there go back to the twelfth century, while the present spacious nave was not begun until 1373. It was dedicated to Christ and the Virgin Mary, and to St. James the Apostle. The church's most precious shrine is that rock-crystal capsule set in a reliquary cross believed to contain drops of the blood of Christ. The capsule is an object of great veneration from the earliest times. Today it is contained in the great Altar of the Holy Blood, which is kept in the upper gallery of the majestic structure, where light from the sun streams in to give radiance to the shrine. Tillman Riemenschneider (1460–1531), the great woodcarver of Wurzburg, made the marvelous altar in 1505. Surely it is one of the most exquisite of all carvings, with the deep feelings of spirituality so amazingly caught by the artist that believing that the whole work was directed by a celestial power is not difficult.

The fifteenth-century high altar is another marvel of beauty. So are Riemenschneider's Altar of St. Francis and the great wood carving of the Altar of the Coronation of the Virgin Mary, the latter standing in front of the end wall of the south aisle. The carving is believed to have been made by Riemenschneider or one of his pupils. While St. Jacob's has been a Lutheran parish church since the Reformation, it is clearly ecumenical in the feelings it evokes both in Catholics and in non-Lutheran Protestants. The poet Kaspar Bruscius in 1557 had advised everyone who could not make a pilgrimage to Jerusalem to see Rothenburg. For the spiritually sensitive, this counsel still has merit.

Just outside the northern walls of Rothenburg is St. Wolfgang's Church, begun in 1475 on the spot where in the old days shepherds would gather to pray and conduct their festivals that blended the spirit of Christ with the old nature religion of the Mother Goddess. The church became a stopping place for pilgrims on their way to Rome or Jerusalem and a place of healing, too, for St. Wolfgang has always been a protector against illness and pests, and a patron and friend of the animals.

On the north side of the nave at St. Wolfgang is Mary's Altar, built in 1480, showing a powerful figure of the Great Mother. Wings were added to this altar depicting scenes of healing by St. Benedict. While this old church is most fascinating to see, with its underground passages and mysterious corners, it is Mary's Altar that carries the vitality to the present moment. I started to leave the altar several times, only to be drawn back by overwhelming vibrations, until while kneeling I felt the special blessing. This is an authentic holy place for healing.

Rothenburg, so widely known for its excellent preservation of medieval architecture, has been spared from destruction through unusual events. During the Thirty Years' War, the commander of the imperial army was determined to raze the town. The burgomaster offered him a cup of the best local wine. The general was moved and agreed to spare the town if some well-known townsman could empty in one draught a six-pint tankard of the same kind of wine. A former amply endowed

72

burgomaster performed the feat. At the north end of the marketplace, this story is re-enacted at the gable clock of the old Ratstrenkstube at certain hours each day.

Several centuries later during World War II, when the Allied forces were ready to attack the town, a native artist whose attractive shop is still near the town center, persuaded the mayor to open the gates rather than have the beautiful town destroyed. Providence moves in mysterious ways, and nothing in the town was destroyed. Rothenburg on the Tauber remains for all to enjoy its medieval splendor.

Not far from Rothenburg is the pilgrimage Church of Our Lord, just a mile out of the little town of Creglingen, in a quiet and pleasant setting. Here the fourteenth-century stone-cut structure contains a magnificent Riemenschneider carving of an altar dedicated to the Virgin Mother.

Tips for Travelers

Rothenburg, the long-time pilgrimage center and walled city on the famous Romantic Road, may be reached by coach from Wurzburg, where frequent train service runs to Frankfurt. The Europabus has a special trip covering much of the Romantic Road from Wurzburg to Fussen.

Rothenburg has a number of good inns, including the Markusturm, which is affiliated with the Romantik Hotels and is located near Markus Gate. The popularity of the town often makes finding accommodations difficult even when they are requested in advance.

Feuchtwangen, some twenty miles south of Rothenburg on the Romantic Road, is a lovely and historic place to stay. The town dates to the ninth century, and has Roman cloisters, well-preserved churches, and pleasant shops. The Greifen-Post Hotel, affiliated with the Romantik group, has a history of six centuries. It is an excellent inn, with beautifully furnished rooms and good meals. Many notables, such as Jenny Lind and Catherine, the wife of the Russian czar, have lodged there.

Picturing Cologne, today the great industrial city of the German Rhineland, as a holy place is difficult unless one lingers awhile in the cathedral and begins to feel the spiritual energies of the early times rising again. In the Middle Ages the city was "holy Cologne," place of pilgrimage and a major theological center of Europe. Such a spiritual heritage is not easily obliterated, not even by the grossness of mammon nor the obscenity of war.

In the first century, when the town was a Roman outpost, a small pagan temple was on the cathedral hill. Some of the walls and remnants of that time remain. Christian groups met in Cologne in the third century, and the next century is associated with the old legend of St. Ursula and the eleven virgins who were murdered by the Huns as they returned from Rome. St. Ursula became the patron saint of the city, whose coat of arms carries eleven flowers for the martyrs beneath the three crowns of the Magi Kings.

The most famous shrine is that of the Three Wise Men, whose relics had been taken by the Empress Helen in the early fourth century to Constantinople, then in later years to Milan. After the fall of that city in 1168, the bones were carried to Cologne. Enveloped in fine embroideries, the remains of those who had followed the light of the great Star to Bethlehem at the time of the Savior's birth were placed in a beautiful shrine in the old Cologne cathedral. They were later placed at the high altar of the great Gothic cathedral begun in 1248. Caspar, Melchior, and Balthazar, as they are often called in the old chronicles, are now in the celestial hierarchy and have been called upon by pilgrims in intercessory prayer for centuries. The great cathedral at Cologne, the largest in Germany and one of the most imposing in all Europe, is dedicated to Christ and His Mother. It is a most appropriate monument for the celebration of the Magi. The three portals of the huge facade open into the five aisles of a majestic interior, with the golden Shrine of the Three Wise Men at the high altar. On either side of the shrine are the pillar statues of Christ and the Virgin. Among the most revered objects are the tenth-century Crucifix of Archbishop Gero and the colorful thirteenth-century "Milan Madonna."

This Gothic structure not only inspires through its magnitude and beauty but evokes feelings of a great period of the past reflecting major spirits who still mightily influence religion today. The cathedral and a number of old churches are closely associated with Cologne's golden age of theology and mysticism in the Middle Ages. Albert the Great, the famous philosopher, preacher, master of the esoteric arts and teacher of Thomas Aquinas, taught there for years. While his bones are in the crypt of St. Andrew's Church, the spirit of Albertus is especially vital today and is known to be present at seances of Christian occultists. Meister Eckhart, spiritual father of the Rhineland mystics and one of the greatest souls in European religious history, preached there. Among his illustrious disciples who studied under him at Cologne were Johannes Tauler, the courageous Dominican preacher, Henry Suso, and Jan van Ruysbroeck. These are the famed Rhineland mystics, those friends of God who opened new channels of communication with the invisible world and who still illumine the thoughts of a myriad of spiritual seekers.

Gerard Groote, the Dutch writer, taught philosophy at Cologne and was spiritually converted while there. The Franciscan theologian Duns Scotus preached in this cathedral, and Nicolas of Cusa had his early training at the university, preparing him for his amazing work in the blending of orthodox Christianity, the new science, and the old occultism. Henry Cornelius Agrippa of Nettesheim, born in Cologne in 1486, became the eminent and controversial physician, theologian, teacher of esoteric doctrines, and practitioner of the old religion. This array of great souls have created such an indelible spiritual influence on the atmosphere of medieval Cologne that all of the materialists of modernity cannot erase it.

Cologne is not only a major railroad center, but being on the Rhine it has various short river excursions available as well as lengthy cruises. The old section of the city has a number of historic churches to view.

Europa Am Dom Hotel, 38 Am Hof, has a good reputation, and is one of several fine hotels near the cathedral.

SALZBURG

Long considered one of the most beautiful cities of Europe, Salzburg is in central Austria not far from the German frontier. Located in a basin about 1,400 feet above sea level near the more northerly slopes of the Alps, it is surrounded by lovely wooded hills, and the River Salzach runs through the heart of the city. The blending of a tradition rich in music and the arts with a natural loveliness makes Salzburg a most attractive place.

A Benedictine abbey was established by St. Rupert around 700 on an ancient site of worship in the old Roman town of Juvavum. This became the cell from which the Christian faith spread throughout the area and is the place where St. Peter's Church has stood for centuries. At the altar of St. Mary is a revered statue of the Virgin, a focal point for healing energies evoked through prayer. At the abbey are catacombs going back to the early days of religious worship, and the graveyard around the church is probably the oldest known burial place in Salzburg province. This picturesque scene is immediately beside the massive Dolomite rock, upon the top of which looms the Hohensalzburg, an eleventh-century castle, which is one of the largest in Europe and a mighty complex of structures which can be seen for miles around.

A short distance across St. Peter's courtyard is the Franciscans' Church, consecrated in 1221 and a site for worship since the eighth century. Within this plain, impressive Romanesque structure, with its huge pillars and the contrasting late-Gothic style of the chancel, is a feeling of being on holy ground, with the unspoiled effect of the architecture and the vibrations of an old unbroken line of worship.

St. Peter's is a short walk from the cathedral, a great baroque Renaissance structure with five aisles and a nave 394 feet long, built from 1614 to 1635 on an ancient holy site where there had been a succession of buildings. St. Rupert and St. Virgil are depicted in handsome statues, along with St. Paul and St. Peter, in front of the main portals. The spiritual influence of the earlier saints was later weakened through a withering of ecclesiastical piety when bishops became princes of the Holy Roman Empire. What these men lacked in spirituality, at least a few gained in architectural genius, for there were some excellent builders among them. Wolf Dietrich von Raitenau, made archbishop in 1587, planned the rebuilding of the cathedral after a fire, wanting to make it bigger than St. Peter's in Rome. His beautiful mistress, Salome Alt, by whom he had twelve children, lived in the chateau of Mirabell on the right bank of the Salzach. This liaison in time brought Wolf Dietrich under the condemnation of the Vatican as being unconducive to the church's aims. His successor, Marcus Sitticus, was a builder, too, erecting the palace at Hellbrunn a few miles out of the city. There he laid out vast gardens with ingeniously constructed water fountains so secretly controlled by the archbishop that they would suddenly go on at the right moment to spray his guests with water. Today's guides are acquainted with these secret methods and delight in spraying unwary tourists. At Hellbrunn, with its vast flower beds and lake, a spring festival is held, opera is performed in the outdoor stone cave theater, and in any season a walk to the lodge at the top of the wooded reservation provides the reward of a marvelous view of Salzburg and the surrounding hills.

The fame of Salzburg is enhanced by its most beloved native son, the great composer Wolfgang Amadeus Mozart

(1756–1791). His father, Leopold Mozart, violinist and composer, often led the chamber music at Mirabell Palace, where today in the same lovely drawing room one can hear the compositions of the Mozarts and the Haydns. Mr. Mozart took his child prodigy on European concert tours and Empress Maria Theresa and her daughter Marie Antoinette heard the boy play his own creations. It would seem that young Mozart, whose operas and symphonies, masses and lyrical pieces are among the finest known in western civilization, enjoyed royal support. However, when he later left Salzburg to dwell in Vienna, he was much neglected and suffered from poverty. In his short life, Mozart composed more great music than any other person. The house where he was born, at 9 Getreidegrasses, is an inspiring place for any music lover to visit. Mozart's family lived on the third floor from 1747 to 1773. Most of the works of his youth were composed here, and in the house one can see his spinet, his violins, his letters and portraits, and a number of his musical compositions. Salzburg today is a world center of classical music, and the annual Mozart festival, conceived by Richard Strauss and others, remains one of Europe's major artistic events. The Festival Hall, with its colorful banners, is located just across the street from the famous old baroque Hors Pond and is widely known, too, as the scene of an exciting moment depicted in the play *The Sound of Music.*

Paracelsus, the great physician, occultist, and spiritual healer, died in Salzburg in 1541, some records indicating that he was killed by jealous enemies. On the right bank of the Salzach one can see the house where he lived, and a short distance beyond is the Church of St. Sebastian, where his body is buried in the portico. After more than four centuries, fresh flowers usually adorn the tomb of Paracelsus. His influence is far greater now than ever, and his spirit in the larger world reaches across the line to this world to help heal people. When one visits St. Sebastian's, one should walk through the cemetery, too, which holds the graves of Mozart's wife and father and a mausoleum that Wolf Dietrich von Raitenau designed for his own grave. The archbishop's personal comment on his life, engraved on the mausoleum and translated into several languages, is very touching to read.

Salzburg is an excellent center for short trips to wooded mountains and quiet lakes, to moated castles and pilgrim churches, and to a variety of spas and healing waters. At Bad Ischl, the famed and fashionable spa of the old imperial days of the Emperor Franz Joseph, the saline waters have been used for curative purposes for centuries. A few miles beyond is St. Wolfgang, a village on the lakeside, where a hermitage chapel in medieval times grew into the fifteenth-century church of today, a long-time place of pilgrimage. Nicholas of Cusa (1401–1464), the great theologian, scientist, and mystic, lived here for several years, his unusual spiritual genius being a real help to all who seek a better understanding of what he called "the unity of contraries." The apparent contradiction of orthodox Christianity, the new science, and the esoteric vanish, Nicholas asserts, and a unity is found when one gets the true perspective.

In the alpine areas of Austria, Bavaria, and Switzerland, something of the old order reflected in spirit and nature remains. It can be felt in the tiny villages and around the mountainside chalets, in the quiet valleys and high on the glaciers. The ancient pattern of the cosmos, apparently changed in urban societies, still persists and gets through to the consciousness in these alpine places. The primitive and ancient view comes into a vivid focus as a much more authentic idea of life than that of our limited technological science. The sensitive pilgrim feels the very merging of time and space, matter and spirit, all becoming as integral parts of the experience of standing on sacred ground. The feeling is intensified at a healing spring in the valley or at a wayside shrine on an alpine path or at a pilgrim church on a wooded hillside. A power rising from Mother Earth sustains and enhances whatever religious manifestations are experienced.

Beautiful Salzburg is a choice city for seeing central Austria and southwestern Bavaria. The main railroad station offers good service to Vienna, which is four hours to the east, or to Innsbruck and Garmisch to the west, or through the Alps south to Italy. The Munich airport is about two hours north.

One-day motor coach trips go to the lovely Konigssee, picturesque Berchtesgaden, and the noted salt mines. Bad Ischl and St. Wolfgang in the lake district constitute another attractive excursion for a day. Twelve miles northeast of Salzburg is Oberndorf, where "Silent Night, Holy Night" was composed and first sung on Christmas Eve in 1818.

During the Salzburg Music Festival, it is necessary to make reservations for tickets and hotels long in advance. The season reaches its height in August. During other times tickets are more easily accessible as are hotel rooms. Many concerts and operas are performed throughout the year, with Mozart sonatas and baroque chamber music played in the halls of the palace and delightful miniature presentations offered at the Marionette Theatre.

Hotel Winkelhofer, 9 Neutorstrasse, is a comfortable, modest, and well-run hotel. The Festival Hall is a pleasant walk of a couple of blocks through the tunnel, and the great churches and the distinctive shops are about the same distance beyond.

VIENNA

Vienna is a great center of history and culture, with many places of religious significance not only in the city itself but within a comfortable driving distance. Less than a mile from St. Stephen's Cathedral, the city's long-time central symbol, may be seen the vast Imperial Palace with its Hofburg Chapel, the great Museum of Fine Arts with its splendid collection of works of the masters, the celebrated State Opera House with its reminders of a golden age of music, and several historic churches such as St. Rupert's and St. Peter's.

Vienna is the musical metropolis of Europe, the home of Franz Schubert and Joseph Haydn, Johannes Brahms and Ludwig van Beethoven, and the senior and junior Johann Strauss. Wolfgang Mozart, residing there for several years, called it "a wonderful place" in a letter to his father. Many say that every season is a musical season in Vienna.

Vindobova is the old name of the settlement from before the time of Christ. A Celtic community was there for perhaps a thousand years before the Christian era. On the right bank of the Danube River, Vindobova was the crossroads then, as today, between the west and the east, with mingled links between German and Magyar and Slav. A Roman garrison stood there for years, and in the Nibelungen legends it is said that Marcus Aurelius, the famous Roman emperor and defender of the old paganism, died there in A.D. 180.

The church of St. Rupert could probably be traced to the late seventh or early eighth century, the present structure being of a few centuries later. It is in the old quarter not far from the Danube Canal. The church is named for Rupert of Salzburg, the missionary bishop who died around 710 and whose widespread travels in German countries probably brought him to Vienna with the Gospel. Believed to be the oldest church in Vienna, St. Rupert's is no doubt built over an ancient pagan shrine. Some believe St. Peter's Church is Vienna's oldest, some contending it was founded by Charlemagne around 800, and others say it dates to an earlier time as a part of a monastery. Historic documents refer to it as the parish church of Vienna. When the plague hit the city in 1679, the emperor vowed that when it passed he would build some great columns to the honor of the Holy Trinity. The columns were erected and later the church was rebuilt, resulting in a beautiful baroque structure.

St. Stephen's Cathedral was consecrated in 1147, and the later Gothic edifice now so widely known and admired arose in the early fourteenth century. The tower, 450 feet high, remains through the years the focal point and symbolic center of Vienna. It is named for the first Christian martyr, who had been stoned to death at the gates of Jerusalem in about A.D. 35. The account is given in chapters six and seven of The Acts of the Apostles, where Stephen is described as "a man full of faith and power" and as one who worked miracles. Later stones were carried from Jerusalem to Vienna and other places, considered by some as relics that had touched the saintly Stephen, who forgave those who killed him. Some traditions relate to visionary appearances of Stephen on the site where the cathedral was built, and through subsequent centuries that saint's intercessory prayers have been often invoked.

Almost as well-known as the tower is the distinctive design of the slanting roof of this cathedral. The interior is lovely, the Virgin's Choir containing a cherished fifteenth-century wood-carved and gilded altarpiece. The high altar of the chancel depicts the stoning of St. Stephen, and nearby is the red marble tomb of Emperor Friedrich III and carvings showing the triumph of good spirits over evil influences.

Vienna is a depository of many valuable and historic art treasures, including religiously significant artifacts from the early ages and venerated relics of Christian origin. Some are found in the Imperial Treasury at the Palace, and in the Historical Museum of Vienna, just across from the spectacular baroque Church of St. Charles at Karlsplatz, where artifacts and ceramics from the Roman and Gothic periods may be seen. The Natural History Museum at Maria Theresien-Platz contains ancient items from the Hallstatt excavations as well as the famous statue of the Venus of Willendorf. This statue, which may be from 12,000 to 20,000 years old, is probably a likeness of the Mother Goddess. Other artifacts that relate to the Mother Goddess from the Lang-Engersdorf excavations at Kornenburg (a few miles northeast of Vienna near the Danube) and that date to 4800 B.C. may be seen.

The eastern section of Austria, along the Danube, is a part of an old European civilization going back thousands of years.

The artifacts being unearthed there and elsewhere in the Balkans reveal the widespread worship of the Great Mother. Statues in limestone and soapstone accent a strong femininity and fecundity, indicating that the goddess is the great seat of power in that ancient European world. Certain areas near the Danube and in the Balkans need to be further explored through psychical means to locate more definitely some of the great power centers that spring from antiquity. Undoubtedly many of the holy places in Austria devoted to the Virgin Mary are the same sites where the Great Goddess of the old religions was worshiped. Under an ancient name or in the guise of the Virgin Mary, the Great Goddess is still worshiped in many village communities of old Europe as well as by pilgrims from near and far who find their way to the shrines.

Many of the lovely baroque pilgrimage churches in Austria contain ancient miracle-working statues that are associated with a tradition of healing and paranormal experiences. For example, some have worshiped the Virgin at the Maria Saal Pilgrimage Church, near Klogenfurt in Carinthia, since around A.D. 600. Deep in the upper Styria mountains in Mariazell, long a popular pilgrimage center where a monk set up a carved statue of Mary in 1157 in a little hut, people found healing, and a church was built. Some of these places appear to have a pre-Christian origin, being holy ground from early times and linked with the worship of this perennial goddess.

Tips for Travelers

The old inner city, within or near the Ringstrasse, is the best place to stay for those who want to be in easy walking distance of the major landmarks. A wide range of hotels is available, from the very elegant and expensive to the comfortable and reasonable, with some good family-run pensions. At 16 Annagasse, between St. Stephen's and the Opera, is the first-class Romischer Kaiser Hotel, associated with the Romantik Hotel chain. It is conveniently located on a quiet street in a small historic building.

Vienna is noted for its pleasant coffee houses, where one can tarry over a sweet roll and coffee without being hurried.

Opera reservations should be made well in advance. Visitors should write ahead to the hotel to reserve tickets.

INNSBRUCK

In the Tyrolean area of Austria is the lovely city of Innsbruck, "the bridge over the Inn" at the foot of the Alps, where the rocky Nordkette ranges form the immediate background. There the Rivers Sill and Inn meet. Innsbruck is one of Europe's great resort and cultural centers, a place especially known for its winter activities and Olympic games. Its origins are old and stem from a strong religious heritage enriched by an ancient mountain mythology.

In Roman times a little settlement called Veldidena was on the route of travel of those crossing the Alps through Brenner Pass. The first mention of this village as Innsbruck was in 1187. A monastery had been there from an early period; some date it to the seventh century. The monks of St. Norbert's order had come in the twelfth century, and perhaps Norbert himself, who traveled widely in France and the Teutonic lands, had preached here. What came to be known as the Abbey of Wilten did come under the leadership of the Premonstratensians, which is St. Norbert's group. In the early history accounts tell of alpine giants associated with the abbey. The Wilten church, a seventeenth-century baroque structure, has statues of the two giants at the entry.

Not far from the monastery is the Pilgrimage Church, now raised to the status of a basilica, which still welcomes pilgrims coming to the venerated statue of the Virgin Mary. The statue stands at the altar, surrounded by four big columns, and the shrine is called that of Our Lady of the Four Columns. Rich art treasures are within, but the screen of separation somehow disturbs the vibrations. No doubt many have had genuine religious experiences there in generations past, and an open sanctuary might well help today's visitors feel the vibrations again.

The basilica is about a mile from the old town, which is a most delightful place to visit. To go from the handsome Maria-Theresienstrasse with the fascinating streets of the old quarter takes one to charming shops, to late medieval buildings such as the legendary Little Golden Roof structure, and to the Hofburg. The latter is the great palace built by Maria Theresa, and the hall of the giants and other state rooms should be visited.

Adjoining the palace is St. James' Cathedral—the baroque structure was built on much older foundations. In early times there was emphasis on the healing power and intercession of St. James the Apostle, who had written in the New Testament how the prayers of a righteous man availeth much and will heal the sick.[1] The painting of Mary by Lucas Cranach the Elder is highly treasured. The princes of earlier times would often take it with them on their travels as a sacred picture exuding protective powers.

Across the corner from the palace is the Hofkirche, a Franciscan church built in the mid-sixteenth century, whose unusually fine statuary reflects a sense of gratitude for the legendary heroes of the faith and the spirits of the holy men of old. For instance, the vast marble mausoleum of the Emperor Maximilian I holds twenty-eight more-than-life-size bronze statues representing the presence of the spirits of the royal personages of yore. And the beautiful Silver Chapel boasts its finely embossed silver statue of the Virgin.

Innsbruck offers much more for the visitor to see, including the splendid Tyrol Folkmuseum. Many places in the nearby area should be enjoyed, such as the beautiful alpine village of Seefeld with a Gothic Parish Church, a place of pilgrimage for centuries, and Stams Abbey, about twenty miles west of Innsbruck in the Upper Inn Valley. This is a magnificent sight, and

[1]James 5:15-16.

the Abbey Church has an altarpiece appropriately representing the Tree of Life, in which are interwoven eighty-four carved figures of the saints around the Virgin. Beyond Stams is historic Imst, and Landeck, with the old castle near the waters of the rushing Inn river and the legends of "the little people."

Understandably, the Tree of Life, from both a mystical biblical view and that of nature's old religion, has unusual symbolic relevance. The great trees of the forest have always been important in the religious traditions, the groves being most ancient as places of worship and prayer. Jacob Grimm, the great German mythologist and scholar, tells how in the Tyrol divine figures are often carved on trees. The Madonna figure was carved on trees in pre-Christian times. Sometimes figures of wonderful maidens or wise old men would be carved sitting inside hollow trees or perched in the branches. "The image of grace" grew up in these Tyrolean groves, becoming in time a part of Christian legend and practice. In the mountains and in the woods these old mysteries still prevail. Whoever ponders these things, especially when enjoying the beauty of the Austrian Alps and the delights of the Tyrolean forests, becomes aware of perennial spiritual powers. The old sacredness remains in the same place, flowing from the presence of God.

Tips for Travelers

Innsbruck is on the main rail lines from Zurich or Garmisch, Salzburg or Vienna. If one is staying in Garmisch or Salzburg, a day's round trip by rail or car would give several good hours for sightseeing in Innsbruck.

One can find an attractive Romantik Hotel in Innsbruck, the Schwarzer Adler, on 2 Kaiserjagerstrasse. It is well-located and has a good Tyrolean and international cuisine.

HELVETIA

One of Europe's most attractive cities, Geneva is situated at the southwest end of the Lake of Geneva, from which flows the waters of the River Rhone. From the shores of this largest lake on the continent one can see Mont Blanc, the highest of Europe's mountain peaks. The city is divided into two parts, separated by the Rhone. The older section is on the left bank.

Geneva was old when Julius Caesar was there in the first century before Christ. The great Roman described the town as being near the old Helvetian border. Lake villages had been situated along the shores in a much earlier time, with evidences of a flourishing life in the Neolithic Age. Celtic tribes, including those known as Helvetii, appeared throughout that considerable area south of the Rhine and from the Jura on the west to the Alps of the south and east. Historic records indicate that the Roman province of Helvetia enjoyed peace and prosperity for several centuries. Toward the end of the Middle Ages, Geneva was under the rule of the Dukes of Savoy and for some time was an independent city. It came under the influence of John Calvin (1509-1564), the French Protestant reformer and brilliant theologian, in 1541, with the establishment of a rigorous theocracy. The city was known as a refuge for persecuted Protestants, but it was a haven limited to those who fitted into Calvin's form of orthodoxy. Tolerance was broader under the subsequent leaders of the theocracy. By the eighteenth century Geneva was a sanctuary for all types of civil, religious, and political refugees, and in time it became Europe's center for international organizations such as the Red Cross, the League of Nations after 1919, and the World Council of Churches.

High on the historic left bank is the Cathedral of St. Peter, the spire of which still remains the most conspicuous landmark of Geneva. In the twelfth and thirteenth centuries when this cathedral was built, princes and peasants joined in the work as an act of faith, and women of nobility and milkmaids united in pushing the wagons carrying the stone and lumber. Historians record how they did so in great procession, with trumpets blowing, hymns being sung, and holy banners waving. With the Reformation in the sixteenth century, the cathedral became the center of Protestant preaching by Guillaume Farel, John Calvin, and their successors. Here, too, were heard the words and tunes of the famous Geneva Psalter, one of the greatest of hymn books.

The pilgrim will find the interior of St. Peter's rather plain, yet the basic Gothic beauty is evident. The chair in which Calvin used to sit in the pulpit may be seen; it is unpretentious and not very comfortable looking. The Princess Emilie of Nassau, daughter of Holland's William the Silent, had taken refuge here with her daughter, and the Nassau Chapel, to the left of the choir, is named in their honor. It is especially set aside and used today as a place for those who wish to meditate and remain in silence. Pilgrims should climb to the north tower for a splendid view. When I climbed to this tower on my first visit to Geneva, I was stirred by the view of the historic city, the great lake, and the more distant Alps. Climbing on foot from the old stone floors up the winding stairs to the tower helps quicken one's thoughts concerning a permanent and permeating spirit that makes for holy ground.

The International Monument of the Reformation, erected in 1917, is an imposing sight, especially with the great stone wall one hundred yards long with a moat of water in front. The four central statues are of Calvin, Farel, Théodore de Béza, and John Knox, the leading reformers of the Calvinist tradition.

Other reformers are honored, too, including Martin Luther and Roger Williams, champion of religious freedom in America.

Many great writers and thinkers have lived in Geneva. Henri Frederic Amiel (1821–1881), the Swiss writer whose *Journal* is a masterpiece of spiritual insight, lived there. A century earlier Geneva was the home of the great Jean-Jacques Rousseau (1712–1778), who was born at 40 Grande Rue and who saw his book *Emile* burned in front of the town hall. Every visitor will want to walk on the little bridge over the Rhone to Rousseau Island and there view the statue of one of the major molders of western thought.

A steamer trip on the Lake of Geneva, known there as Lac Léman, is a delightful way to visit some of the lovely little towns on both the Swiss and French sides of the lake. The lake has many piers, and one can take a variety of trips. Wherever one boards, one can see the 400-feet-high Jet D'Eau, shooting up from the lake, and it will remain in sight for miles after the boat leaves port.

Coppet is eight miles from Geneva and makes a good stop on a boat trip. There may be seen the lovely chateau of Madame Germaine de Staël (1766–1817), that brilliant French writer and friend of freedom who courageously maintained her opposition to Napoleon's exploitations and helped keep intellectual liberty alight.

About five miles beyond Coppet is the charming town of Nyon, founded two thousand years ago and possessing an old castle by the shore and some Roman columns in the park. Nyon is the birthplace of the saintly theologian of the Wesleyan movement, John William Fletcher (1729–1785), later of Madeley, England.

A longer excursion by boat would provide time to see Lausanne, with its old section and the beautiful Gothic Cathedral of Our Lady. Lausanne was long a favorite resort of the old world royalty. For years the cathedral was a place of pilgrimage, the statue of the Virgin being venerated and associated with healing miracles.

Geneva has a major international airport and railroad station, with good connections for leading cities of Europe. It is a good base for seeing western Switzerland and the French Alps and holds fine opportunities for visiting the charming towns along the shores of Lac Léman. The excursion boats stop at both the Swiss and French piers. The best way to explore the old section of Geneva is by foot.

The Hotel Bristol, at 10 rue du Mont-Blanc, on the right bank and in the center of the city, is less than a block from the lake. It is a long-established, well-maintained hotel, with pleasant rooms and good food.

LAUTERBRUNNEN VALLEY

Any search for the Garden of Eden would sooner or later lead to the Lauterbrunnen Valley in the Bernese Oberland of Switzerland. In the Biblical Eden, where man and woman first dwelt on the earth, no sickness existed, as Adam and Eve had a right relationship with God, a harmony of spirit and body amid an environment made lovely through the vibrations of peace and beauty and health.

All of us feel a nostalgia for paradise, a desire to recover wholeness, to find harmony with the Divine, to experience peace rather than strife, orderliness rather than discord, loveliness rather than ugliness, purpose rather than meaninglessness. Our spirit and thought help to create such an Eden, and in certain places the cooperating energies—what we sometimes call the good vibrations—blend and give us peace. The spirits of nature, the elements and elementals, are ripe for helping when we have a right receptivity and responsiveness. At such times and in such places the healing power is received. Time and space, spirit and matter, seem as one, and the experience of a certain place becomes full of a mysterious, animating influence creating felicity and serenity. We feel the enchantment, and while we cannot explain it, we know it is real and it is good. We are in a paradise. This can describe our experience in the Lauterbrunnen Valley.

The wonderful and long-time resort town of Interlaken, so called from its position between the lakes of Thun and Brienz, is eight miles from the little village of Lauterbrunnen, at the entry to the magical valley. A good road runs between the two, and the Bernese Oberland Railway may be taken from the east station of Interlaken to Lauterbrunnen, where cable car and electric train connections may be made for such alpine villages as Murren, Scheidegg, and Grindelwald. The white, fast-moving Lütschine River, with tributaries from glaciers and springs, keeps the narrow valley green and perennially cool, even in the midst of summer. The very name of Lauterbrunnen is derived from the many streams, luter meaning "clear" and brunnen meaning "springs." The many waterfalls, like sprays from the precipices high above the valley, together with the even higher glacier-covered peaks beyond give the area an awe-inspiring beauty. Most prominent of the falls is the Staubbach, whose waters resemble a lace veil dropping a thousand feet. Lord Byron refers to the Staubbach as the "pale courser's tail" of the Apocalypse. These falls inspired the great Goethe, whose poem about them was later set to music by Franz Schubert.

A charming walk of about two miles takes the visitor from the little village church through the meadows, with cattle and sheep grazing around an occasional flower-boxed chalet, and up to a most impressive and unusual natural sight, Trummelbach Falls. These falls are fed by the snows of the great Alps, of the Jungfrau, Eiger, and Monch, peaks more than 13,000 feet in elevation. The falls are inside a cavernous gorge and have been described as "nature's own power house." One of the falls shoots out horizontally from a great rock with tremendous force and a resounding roar. Standing in the great gorge, with its closeness to the inner powers of Mother Earth, is an unforgettable experience.

By cable and electric railway one can ascend to Murren, which is 5,400 feet high and beautifully situated on the top of precipices above the Lauterbrunnen Valley. Murren has marvelous mountain vistas. When the famous American preacher, the widely traveled Phillips Brooks, attended services at the little church in Murren a century ago, he heard the pastor call it the most splendidly situated church in Christendom. And Brooks wrote home, "I rather think he was right."

The trip from Murren up to the Schilthorn, which is 9,754 feet high, affords visitors remarkable panoramic views. Wengen is a lovely village far above the valley on the opposite side from Murren. No sight is more beautiful than viewing the Jungfrau from near the spire of the Wengen church. In this Lauterbrunnen area an element in the very atmosphere casts a spell of enchantment. It is the homeland of Alpine Gods and Goddesses, and a cherished rendezvous for seekers of nature's mystic wonders.

Interlaken, with its lovely old inns, charming walks, interesting shops, and magnificent views, is an ideal place to see the Bernese Oberland. The town goes back to the twelfth century, when an Augustinian monastery became the center for religious worship. In the same pleasant vicinity today are two churches, the older one Protestant, the newer one Roman Catholic, whose towers give the impression from a distance of one building because they stand so close together on the ancient and hallowed ground.

Trains leave Interlaken from both the east depot and the west one, and excursion boats ply to entrancing ports on both Lake Thun and Lake Brienz. A train can take one through majestic scenery to the little village of Sachseln, about halfway between Interlaken and Lucerne. The parish church here contains the grave and relics of St. Nicolas von der Flüe (1417–1487), the farmer turned hermit and an unusual visionary. He was a devotee of the Virgin Mary, who often appeared to him, and was one of the beloved folk heroes of Switzerland. For years his only food and drink were the elements of Holy Communion. When representatives of warring cantons appealed to the mystic in 1481, he brought about a peace plan acceptable to all. Nicolas is looked upon today as the spiritual father of the Swiss Confederation and its policy of neutrality.

Tips for Travelers

The Swiss railroads are excellent, clean and punctual, with a well-run system covering all main places in the country. Whether by rail, motor coach, or automobile, one can leave the Zurich airport and be at Interlaken in about three hours.

Interlaken, as from the days of its famed royal visitors, remains a splendid center for seeing the Bernese Oberland. It is only eight miles from the Lauterbrunnen Valley. Trains leave Interlaken regularly for Lauterbrunnen and other alpine points and connect with cable cars for the Jungfraujoch, Schilthorn, and other great mountain peaks. Interlaken has two railway stations, and steamer excursions run on the two lakes.

The Beau Rivage is a beautiful nineteenth-century-type hotel, with flower gardens in the front and rooms with balconies to view the Jungfrau and the glorious Alps. The cuisine is excellent. The hotel is on the famous drive, Höheweg, and is a short distance from the stations and the dock.

In the Lauterbrunnen Valley, for those who wish to be closer to the mountains, are many pleasant little hotels of the chalet type, such as the Staubach in Lauterbrunnen, as well as ones higher in the Alps at Murren and Wengen.

ZURICH

The largest city in Switzerland, spreading out on both banks of the Limmat River and along the foot of Lake Zurich, is very old. Lake-dwellers were the earliest inhabitants on these shores, going back centuries before Christ, and a Helvetian settlement was thriving there when the Romans took control in 58 B.C. Christianity was introduced in the late second and early third century.

Charlemagne founded the cathedral on the right bank of the Limmat around A.D. 800, and a half century later on the other side of the river the monastery of Our Lady was established by Ludwig the German. Zurich played an important role in the development of the Swiss Confederation, of which it became a part in 1351. During the Reformation, Ulrich Zwingli (1484–1531), priest, professor, and Protestant reformer, preached a rather extreme new Gospel in Zurich. In time the city became an international trade and banking center. Cultural leadership characterizes the city today. Heinrich Pestalozzi, the noted educationalist, was born there in 1746, and Carl Jung, the psychologist, established his center there in the twentieth century.

The cathedral, more often called Gross-Münster, is the most imposing structure of the city, its eleventh-century architecture being a clear example of a plain Romanesque style. It has two western towers, one bearing a statue of Charlemagne, its founder. The church was dedicated to three Christian missionary-martyrs of the third century—Saints Felix, Regula, and Exuperantius, considered the patron saints of Zurich. Their graves, under one of the chapels, have long been revered as holy ground. The nave has some fine old bas-relief pieces, and in the crypt is the original statue of Charlemagne. The more modern bronze doors contain some very striking Biblical scenes. Services have been in the Protestant tradition since the Reformation.

The Church of Our Lady, the Frau Münster, is on the left bank and is dedicated to the Virgin Mary. Founded in the ninth century for the work of nuns, the church today appears in its thirteenth-century architectural beauty. Ludwig the German (804–876), also called Louis, founder of the German kingdom and a staunch defender of the Christian Faith, established this center for nuns. His devout daughter, Hildegard, was the first abbess. Modern frescoes in the lovely cloisters depict scenes from the life and healing work of Hildegard and her followers.

A short distance from the Frau Münster is the medieval parish church of St. Peter, built upon the site of an ancient pagan holy place. The tower contains one of the largest clocks in Switzerland. Johann Kaspar Lavater (1741–1801), the noted mystic and poet, was pastor there for twenty-three years and his body is buried in the church.

From the shores of Lake Zurich or from the wooded heights above the city the glorious Alps loom on clear days. The trip is not long to the wonders of the mountains, to many places of deep religious association, to beautiful Lucerne, to old pilgrimage churches, and to mysterious Mount Pilatus with its awe-inspiring vistas.

Lucerne, thirty-six miles from Zurich, grew from an eighth-century Benedictine monastery and is one of the most superbly located cities of Europe. Located at the foot of the Lake of Lucerne, on both sides of the River Reuss, and in the midst of wooded hills and great mountains, the city itself is charming. The picturesque Kapell-Brücke, the roofed wooden bridge across the river, goes back to 1333. Hanging from the rafters of the bridge as one crosses are 112 paintings done around 1600, telling the story of the lives of the early patron saints and folk heroes of the area. Lucerne has some lovely churches. The visitor will also want to see the famous Lion Monument, designed by the noted Danish sculptor Bertei Thorvaldsen (1768–1844). On the shores of the lake a little more than a mile from the town is the country villa of Tribschen, where Richard Wagner lived for several years and which was later the home of the great opera singer Minnie Hauk (1852–1929). It is now owned by the city and is a museum.

A visit to Mount Pilatus, about 7,000 feet in elevation, is a memorable experience. One can ascend by cogwheel railway, and the more adventurous may wish to descend in a four-passenger cable gondola. The old tradition holds that the mountain is named for Pontius Pilate because his body, having been rejected in other places of the old world, finally found a resting place in a little lake in the mountain. His spirit is believed to dwell on this mountain and to be linked with the elementals causing the gathering of storm clouds. From Mount Pilatus the views of the vast Bernese Oberland are magnificent, except when Pilate is unhappy and stirs up a storm.

Tips for Travelers

Zurich, with its frequent air and rail connections, is the major center for sightseeing in Switzerland. One-day trips by coach, car, or rail can be made to Lucerne, Einsiedeln, Basle, and the beautiful capital city of Berne. The latter is another excellent base for sightseeing.

In Zurich, the Glockenhof at 31 Sihlstrasse, with its pleasant garden court and quiet central location, has a good reputation. A little farther from the business district is the large and modern Nova Park Hotel, 420 Badenerstrasse, consisting of several buildings, a garden cafe, and an array of services. Quick and frequent transportation takes travelers to the heart of the city.

For those who want more time in the mountains staying closer to Lucerne or Interlaken is better.

EINSIEDELN

Saint Meinrad was born in southern Swabia during the later years of the reign of Charlemagne (about A.D. 800). He was the Count of Hohenzollern, and after entering the priesthood, he taught for a time at a school on the shores of Lake Zurich. Retiring to the Etzel Pass in 828 to live as a hermit, he later moved to a more remote place in the wooded hills, where he built his little hermitage. He spent his days tilling the soil and praying for the sick and needy. One cold wintry day in January 861 he was murdered by robbers, an act witnessed by his friends the ravens who followed the culprits so noisily into town they aroused the people to apprehend the evil-doers.

98

Meinrad's cell in the forest became holy ground, and a center of monastic life. By 934 an abbey had been established there.

From these beginnings the great pilgrimage center of Einsiedeln grew and became the foremost healing shrine of Europe. The focal object is the carved statue of the Virgin Mary, often called the Black Madonna because it has been darkened by the constant burning of votive candles through the centuries. People have various views concerning the origin of the sacred statue, one tradition holding that it had been given to St. Meinrad in 853 by Hildegard, daughter of Ludwig the German and abbess of Zurich.

This wooden figure, slightly smaller than life-size, is now painted strawberry red and gold, with the face and hands remaining an ebony black, and is generally bedecked and ornamented. Certainly, it has been the central reminder of devotion to the Great Mother for the many centuries of pilgrimages to Einsiedeln. She is the real heart of this forest community, the vital center of the long history of the abbey, and the giver of hope and healing and new life to pilgrims.

From early times the shrine has contained the hermit's cell. A marble canopy was erected in 1617, the shrine being within the later structure of the abbey church. The present edifice, dating from the seventeenth century, is a marvelous work of baroque style.

As one approaches Einsiedeln today, the vast abbey looms in quiet beauty amid the hills and adjoining woods, with its hotels and shops spreading out in the foreground. The little curio stores form a semicircle close to the entry, and for some people this is distracting. There is no interference, however, with the central location of the golden Madonna fountain, where devout visitors drink from the twelve spiggots, perhaps mindful of the old tradition that at this holy well the Lord Jesus was seen drinking the water and blessing it.

Ascending the steps, vast in width beyond the fountain, one can see the statue of St. Meinrad above the facade. Upon entering the abbey, one sees the Shrine of Mary, the glorious

Black Madonna. Whoever inwardly prepares for the experience is not apt to forget it. This shrine, according to a time-honored tradition, was consecrated by angels at the command of Christ. Healing is associated with the pilgrimages of the centuries, with great numbers cured of a variety of sicknesses from the earliest visits, and since 1338 records have been kept of many of the supernormal activities. It is reported that in 1466 130,000 pilgrims came to the shrine in a single fortnight, from as far away as the Baltic Sea in the north and the Mediterranean in the south. People come today, as in the past, to pray at the miraculous statue of the Black Madonna, and many find healing and renewal.

While the surrounding area is beautiful, and the interior of the spacious baroque structure exceptionally lovely with many attractive art works and interesting niches, the pilgrim is constantly being drawn back to the Black Madonna. She reigns, and her shrine is the powerful magnet. The presence of the surrounding hosts of heaven can be felt few places as strongly as there.

I have been at Einsiedeln on a number of occasions, and each time I find a fresh blessing. One of the most memorable hours of my life occurred there, when the magnetic power of the Madonna was so great that I could not move away from the shrine. I knelt in meditation and in a few moments was in another dimension of life and consciousness. All of those folk I loved so much, parents and relatives and friends, including many parishioners who had passed on, were present, like an encompassing cloud of witnesses. They were more vivid than when they were in their physical bodies; they were clearer than any life here. It was an exalted experiencing of what the creeds call "communion of saints," only it was highly personal and seemed totally free of all sectarian differences. Protestants, Catholics, and those I have known of other religious backgrounds were present in the vivid joys of this visionary experience of reality. I do not know how long it lasted, but when I was back in this world again I felt as though I was still partly in paradise.

Believing that water from the fountains is charged with holy propensities, I always bring back some to the states, as do my friends. One friend in particular, from Illinois, had a diagnosed malignancy in one eye and was prepared to have an operation. He called me about it, and I suggested that at a set time, he should wipe his eye with the Einsiedeln water, at the same time that I would pray for him. This he did, and when he returned to the hospital for the operation, the doctors were amazed that the growth had disappeared and he had been healed.

Einsiedeln is a peace center, too. During World War II, great numbers came to the Black Madonna to pray that Switzerland would be kept out of the hostilities. Following the war, many came for thanksgiving to the Great Mother, who had kept them in the secure folds of peace. People still come to pray for peace and goodwill among men and nations, as they come with their requests for healing. It is interesting to note that one of the most remarkable of all healers, the great Paracelsus, was born in Einsiedeln in 1490. A short distance from the entry to the abbey is a handsome monument of Paracelsus as a child with his mother.

Pilgrims of the Roman tradition must find it inspiring to be met by the monks in procession, headed by the carriers of the cross, the banner, and sacred relics, and be thus led to the holy place. But Protestants and other spiritual pilgrims find equal inspiration. The place is not really sectarian at all; it is universally recognized as holy ground, with the particular monks present acting in a sort of custodial capacity. The shrine is open to all who come, and every responsive pilgrim finds a blessing in the Mother of all.

Tips for Travelers

The pilgrimage center of Einsiedeln has some good local inns near the shrine, as well as a number of attractive places to eat.

For one staying in Zurich, the train service is good, with

several departures each day, and the trip takes a little more than an hour. Upon arriving in Einsiedeln, one has a pleasant walk from the depot through the village, with its woodcarving shops and other stores, to the fountain and the abbey. A walk into the nearby and partially wooded hills, which offer a lovely view of the abbey, can be an inspiring experience.

DORNACH

The area around Basle has been related to universal spiritual movements from the early centuries. The Friends of God, devoted to the old prophetic tradition of St. Hildegarde, the twelfth-century sibyl of the Rhine, had its center in the Basle area. The fourteenth-century mystic Johann Tauler and his contemporary Jan van Ruysbroeck, both disciples of Meister Eckhart and associated with Rhineland mysticism, lived awhile in this section.

The town of Dornach, only four or five miles south of Basle, has a distinctive role in the modern world and the civilization of the future because of the Goetheanum there, from which emanates the continuing influence of Rudolf Steiner (1861–1925), the great philosopher, educator, clairvoyant prophet, and most amazing spiritual genius. The place is alive today with classes and activities, and with students and visitors from many parts of the world. While the architecture of the structures is unusual and attracts interest, it is only in one's appreciation of Steiner's spirit that the place has its real appeal.

Dornach itself has some significant forerunners in the spiritual approach to life, so it is not accidental that Steiner accepted property here to build his center in 1913.

Rudolf Steiner, born in Austria and educated in Vienna, became a foremost authority on Goethe and a leading philosopher whose lectures and activities in Germany and throughout Europe led to the formation of the movement called Anthroposophy. This may be described as a path of knowledge leading the spiritual in man to the spiritual in the universe. Steiner developed a new form of education, involving fresh approaches to the humanities, mathematics, natural sciences, and psychical research. He stimulated therapeutic methods of thought and movement to help the retarded, new methods for medicine and agriculture, and fresh ways to cooperate with the spirits of nature in healing and learning. His understanding of creative arts became a major contribution, particularly in the development of what is called eurythmy, which blends dance-like movements with mind, music, and speech.

Steiner's dream had been to lay the foundation of a new civilization, wherein he could see the blending of eastern and western cultures in the deeper meaning of the Christ. Individuals, with their distinctive spiritual gifts, unite in a common work for good, fitting creatively and well into a divine purpose. That this can be done even amid trying times is witnessed during the tragic war years of 1914–1918 when people from seventeen nationalities worked together peacefully, building the Goetheanum, the name given to Steiner's school of spiritual science. While the first structure, so carefully planned, was destroyed by fire, Steiner set the next plans for a new building into motion prior to his departure for the eternal world. His last days and moments at Dornach were spent in his study at the foot of his own great statue of Christ.

The rather fantastic appearance of the present Goetheanum, with its concrete domes and pillars, colored glass and paintings, shows in architectural form what Goethe had perceived in nature: a harmonious order in which living forms develop from one another. For an unusual experience, walk through the corridors of this vast structure, visit the book store and library, view the art objects, watch the eurythmy practice in the auditorium, and mingle with students and teachers of various ages and backgrounds. Today Waldorf Schools teach the Steiner way in many parts of the world, and Steiner publishing houses in Europe and America provide a steady flow of books and pamphlets written by the great spiritual philosopher and his followers.

Anyone interested in the deeper aspects of Christian esoteric thought and innovative ideas on education and the arts would find a visit to Dornach not only fascinating but perhaps a time for a new insight in the spiritual mysteries.

Tips for Travelers

While very close to Basle, with its great cathedral and university, Dornach may be reached in a one-day round trip from Berne, Interlaken, Geneva, or Zurich. Vegetarian meals are served in the Goetheanum restaurant, in a separate building a short distance from the main edifice.

For a visit to Dornach one should write in advance to The Goetheanum School of Spiritual Science, Dornach, Switzerland.

THE
LOWLANDS

An independent and industrious people have long dwelt in that area of the continent bordering France and Germany and the North Sea. Known as the low countries, this flat northerly land, with some hills and mountains farther south, is now called Belgium, Holland, and Luxembourg. French and Dutch are spoken, commerce is prosperous, the arts flourish, and charming towns and a picturesque countryside characterize much of this compact area. Diverse spiritual power centers are found, some origins going back to ancient tribes and enhanced by an early Christian mystical witness.

The banks of the great River Schelde at Antwerp are where the main action of the *Lohengrin* traditions took place during the first half of the tenth century. A nameless knight, described in the old legends as "the hero from on high" who seems "from heaven descended," arrives in response to the prayers of Elsa. He comes in a boat drawn by a wonderful swan. When the knight proposes marriage, Elsa is told she must never ask the knight's name and where he comes from. After her lost brother is restored, Elsa insists the knight tell her his name, and Lohengrin then leaves her. The swan boat carries him back to the holy mountain where the Holy Grail is hidden. All the mysteries of the old religions, of the dark magic and the perennial light, are depicted in the *Lohengrin* legend. The words and music for this great opera by Richard Wagner are a superb portrayal of the ancient story. There are reasons why the mystery drama is so closely associated with Antwerp. A strange sacredness marks the blending of the river and the land where one of Europe's greatest cathedrals stands and where master artists received their inspiration. In the quest for the Holy Grail, in seeking that essence of life that restores the lost paradise, one finds some clues in Belgium's Antwerp.

The one "from heaven descended" had stood on sacred ground where the Deity had been worshiped from earliest times. Three centuries after Lohengrin's arrival, the Cathedral of Our Lady was begun in 1352. More than two hundred years in the building, the magnificent edifice arose above the banks of the Schelde, and its spire, more than 400 feet high, is seen for many miles along the mighty river. The entry, with its fine statuary, opens into a nave of majestic beauty and reaches a climax at the high altar with its incomparable painting by Peter Paul Rubens of the Assumption of the Virgin. The cathedral has many other treasures and inspired sights, such as the vista looking upward to the tiered towers or Rubens' panels on either side of the nave depicting the Elevation of the Cross and the Descent from the Cross. Only Rubens could portray the death of Christ, the darkest moment of history, and at the same time reveal the transcendent joy of what it truly means: eternal life.

I have visited this cathedral a number of times, the most memorable being one evening when my wife and I, after an afternoon boat trip along one of the largest harbors in the world, walked to the square and found the cathedral doors open and a concert by a youth symphony from Amsterdam about to begin. As we sat in the great nave, with the graves of those of other centuries under the stones beneath our feet, the music filling our ears, and the Rubens paintings before us, we were strongly aware of an encompassing cloud of witnesses and the Queen of Heaven giving her blessing.

A landmark of unusual interest in Antwerp is the Museum Plantin-Moretus. Here the great printer Christopher Plantin (1514–1589) published the Bible in various languages, Latin and Greek Classics, and scholarly works of Roman Catholics and Protestants, including many secret mystical manuscripts.

As a young man he decided to make his home in Antwerp, writing Pope Gregory XIII that he felt the very place shone with an aura of love for the faith. Plantin made a great contribution to both scholarship and religious freedom, as well as to esoteric thought. His son-in-law, John Moretus, and the family descendants continued the work for more than 300 years. The richly filled libraries, with the Gutenberg Bible, rare manuscripts, paintings and drawings by the Flemish masters, woodblocks, copper-plates, and other treasures, are a part of this historic structure. It is certainly one of the most remarkable museums of its kind in existence.

Antwerp, as the home of Peter Paul Rubens (1577–1640), is one of the world's most superb art centers. Works of this most prolific of all great artists may be seen not only in the Museum of Fine Arts and in the Cathedral but in several other great churches of Antwerp, including St. Charles Borromeo's, St. Augustine's, and St. Jacob's. At the altar of the latter is the artist's tomb and his painting of the Madonna and the Saints, which is perhaps his last work and which he wanted placed there. In it are those dear to his heart—his first wife as Mary Magdalene, his second wife as the Madonna, his father as St. Jerome, and himself as St. George—reminding viewers that he wanted to be remembered as a defender of the Christian faith.

Rubens' house is a great place to visit. The old materials of the original house have been used in later years to reconstruct the wonderful edifice the artist had built on property he purchased in 1610. The lovely gardens are there, and the statues in the inner court show his view of the Bible and of the Greek and Roman hierarchy of the Gods. Inside are a few of his works, including the famed *Cimon and Pero* painting, as well as some by Jordaens. Among Rubens' many students, Anthony Van Dyck and Jacob Jordaens are probably the best known. In Rubens' remarkable life one may see not only a quest for the Holy Grail but a certain sustaining joy of one who had already experienced the reality of paradise. Rubens went to mass early every morning, feeling this religious experience must precede any touch of his brush to the canvas.

His far-flung travels not only as an artist but as a diplomat amid turbulent times were done in heartfelt efforts for peace in Europe. His love for Christ and for Mary and his abiding affection for the perennial gods and goddesses is magnificently shown in his works. His two marriages, to Isabella and to Helene, were exceedingly happy, and his paintings of feminine beauty, amid sylvan scenes of joyousness, are really glimpses into a transcendent world where all's well. In Rubens one finds a recovery of the everlasting Eden.

Tips for Travelers

Antwerp is on the Trans Europe Express, with fast rail service to Amsterdam, Brussels, and Paris. The depot is next to the delightful Antwerp Zoo.

The city has many good hotels, such as De Keyser, at 66 DeKeyseriei, and the Waldorf, 36 Belgielei, as well as lesser known ones catering to the Flemish. Antwerp has fine shopping districts and some little stores, dealing in pewter, lace, and art works in the old section around the cathedral.

A boat trip on the River Scheldt is a good way to see the great harbor and to enjoy vistas of the city and countryside. The excursion boats' wharf is near the old Castle Steen, with its gigantic statue in front, and inside the fine Maritime Museum. Another good trip is to visit nearby Middelheim Park, adorned with many modern pieces of sculpture and which has a lovely place to dine in the chateau.

BRUGES AND GHENT

A somewhat flattened and elongated triangle in Flanders connects Antwerp with Ghent and Bruges. The spiritual centers of these three cities may well be linked by the cross-currents of ley-lines beneath the earth's surface, or perhaps by what has been called by older mystics as paths of the angels of the arts. While the ancient territory called Flanders fluctuated in size, it included that coastal region extending from Calais in the west to the River Schelde in the east. In the medieval period there were two parts, with Bruges the center of one and Ghent the other.

Ghent had a monastic center in the seventh century, and a city of beauty and commerce developed in the subsequent generations. The river Lys and other streams and canals make for a place of many islands on which still stand a variety of picturesque buildings. It is a fascinating city to explore, with the grim old Castle of the Counts of Flanders, the many churches and belfries, and the secluded *beguinages* on their islands. The *Beguines* is a name given to religious women who under special vows are grouped together in quiet enclosed areas for meditation, the care and healing of the sick, and such crafts as lace-making and weaving. They controlled their own property, and, while devout in their faith and work, were often independent in their convictions. These women were often deeply mystical and were sometimes considered by the Vatican to be heretical. Their centers, particularly in Ghent and Bruges, were spiritually powerful in the old days, and their strength for good is still felt today.

Of the many splendid churches in Ghent, of particular note is the Cathedral of St. Bavon. The present structure dates largely from the fifteenth century, although the crypt dates to 400 years earlier. Many art treasures decorate the cathedral, including the noted polyptych by Hubert and Jan van Eyck, called the *Adoration of the Lamb.* This religious masterpiece has miraculously survived fire, theft, and vandalism over a period of centuries.

Bruges is first mentioned in written records in 892, although a settlement existed there from much earlier times. About five miles from the North Sea, this colorful walled city on the river Zwin was at its height during the thirteenth and fourteenth centuries, and as a major medieval trade center, it was influenced by the Teutonic Hanseatic league. The city withstood ravages in later times, and it is providential that its unsurpassed beauty as a medieval town has survived essentially intact to the present. A center of Flemish painting, Bruges remains one of the chief art cities of Europe.

If one arrives by train, a walking tour will soon open one's eyes to a place of charm. Beginning at the depot, one crosses a canal and then walks to the Minnewater, turning to saunter along its sides to the enchanting area of the old Béguinage, home of the religious women. Here the continuing flavor of medieval times is felt, and continuing along the canal one is soon at the twelfth-century St. John's Hospital, which is still quietly directed by the Augustinian nuns. One of the rooms contains six paintings by the great Hans Memling, master of the old Flemish school of the arts. Entering this place so long associated with prayer, healing, and beauty and so influenced by the mystic works of this old master is an inspiring experience.

Just across the street is the Church of Our Lady, founded by St. Boniface in 875. The present structure dates to 1210. It has a tremendous tower of 375 feet, begun in the late thirteenth century, and the interior is rich in art works. The most famous treasure is Michelangelo's white marble statue of the Virgin and Child, which stands on the altar of the most southern nave. The atmosphere of this area of Bruges is filled with a spirit both mystical and exalted.

A few blocks beyond, along streets often bedecked with colorful banners, today's pilgrims come to the Basilica of the Holy Blood as those of old. This unusual edifice consists of two superimposed chapels—St. Basil's on the ground level and that of the Holy Blood above. Relics from the Holy Land were brought in 1150 and placed in this chapel. The reliquary is believed by some to contain drops of the Blood of Christ, which has attracted pilgrims and tourists for centuries. An elaborate procession travels along the main streets every year on the first

Monday following the second of May. Nearby and facing the market looms the famed Belfry of Bruges, 255 feet above the walk, with its great carillon.

When the American poet Henry Wadsworth Longfellow was there in 1842, he wrote in his journal: "The chimes seemed to be ringing incessantly, and the air of repose and antiquity was delightful . . . Oh, those chimes, those chimes! how deliciously they lull one to sleep."

Later Longfellow recalled his experience in his poem, "The Belfry of Bruges," writing:

> Visions of the days departed, shadowy
> phantoms filled my brain,
> They who live in history only seemed to
> walk the earth again.

Elements of sacredness are felt in so many ways in Bruges, not only in these noted landmarks but in the Church of Our Lady of the Potterie, with its long tradition of healing at the venerated statue of Mary, and in the many art works of Jan van Eyck and Roger van de Weyden, Hans Memling, Gerard David, and the other religious painters of the old Flemish school. The pilgrim of today finds a magical quality in Bruges and when leaving realizes, like the poet, that "hours had passed away like minutes."

Tips for Travelers

Good and frequent rail service runs from Antwerp to Ghent and Bruges, as do motor coach excursions. A full day is needed for even a minimal visit to either of these rare cities. Both cities have some lovely small inns. Late information regarding lodging is regularly available through the Belgian National Tourist Office. In Bruges a slow walking tour is recommended as the best way to see this fascinating town and its canals, and to feel something of the vibration of some of the holy places.

113

A thickly populated area where there had been a settlement from time immemorial, Holland has a strong spiritual element felt in some unexpected places. A long tradition of regional planning and remarkable feats of engineering have reclaimed large sections of land from the ocean. Certainly, a distinctive spiritual power coming from a blend of earth and sea has mightily influenced the life of this area of the lowlands. Quite beyond its well-known commerce and its Rotterdam harbor, the largest in the world, and a long history of globe encircling navigation, the country is characterized by a flourishing of the arts, by its flowers and simple natural beauty, by the neatness and compactness of its appearance, and by an almost proverbial reputation for a fulfillment of Wesley's famed dictum "cleanliness is next to godliness."

Perhaps nothing is more precious in this monarchial land than Holland's long-time openness to freedom of thought and expression. While bitter wars of intolerance were fought in Reformation times, there followed centuries of comparative freedom. From King Frederick V of Bavaria in the early seventeenth century to Kaiser Wilhelm II of Germany, who dwelt in exile at Doorn Castle from 1918 to 1941, many have found refuge in Holland. Then, too, the Pilgrims who were to settle New England found an early haven in Holland. The spiritual influence of men like Erasmus, Coornhart, and Arminius and of the Brethren of the Common Life surely reflect a spirit of freedom that seems to permeate the Dutch atmosphere.

Groups of mystics, scholars, and humanists gathered in various parts of Holland through the centuries, and their influence is not easily confined to any one place. In this small country, Amsterdam, with its own attractiveness, makes an ideal center for today's pilgrims.

A most magnetic city, Amsterdam was originally a small fishing village on the Amstel River. The city derived its name from the Amstel, where a dam was built to prevent floods from the Zuiderzee tides. As Amsterdam grew through the centuries, the many canals spread out in a great fanshape. The city has more than fifty canals and a hundred or more islands linked by more than 400 bridges, water long being the major means of transportation. With the city's origins being traced to the inflow of waters, one can conclude an ancient linkage with the worship of the Water Goddess. While other towns in Holland were founded even earlier, Amsterdam is today's major center for the usual sightseeing. Because of the compactness of the country it can also serve as a good base for the one who seeks the atmosphere of the mystical. Beguine houses from the fourteenth century, several historic churches, and places associated with some of the greatest artists and philosophers of Europe are an integral part of the Amsterdam tradition.

St. Willibrord, the Northumbrian missionary, had come around 640 to Luxembourg and to Utrecht, where he became bishop. He won many converts, although he was unsuccessful in winning his friend, Radbod, the famous leader of the old northern heathenism. During the next several centuries small Christian groups grew in the area along with the continuing of the old religion. The first recorded mention of the town as Amsterdam is in a charter dated 1275.

The oldest church in the city is called the Oude Kerk, or the Old Church, was consecrated in 1306, and was dedicated to St. Nicholas. Not only has it been a worship center ever since, but it has long been a focal point for community and social activity. In the sixteenth century a fine tower 223 feet high was built. The church held cherished relics before the Reformation, and it had been a place of healing. It stands in the oldest part of the city, within a few feet of the red light district. What an unusual phenomenon today to find Amsterdam's oldest church surrounded by practitioners of the oldest profession.

In 1347 a chapel was founded in the Kalverstraat, now a shopping center near the dam, and it came to be known as the Chapel of "the Miracle of Amsterdam." A misplaced wafer of the Holy Sacrament appeared indestructable when it was not consumed by fire, and a series of unusual incidents pertaining to the consecrated wafer followed. A century later King Maximilian I of Austria, who became a Holy Roman Emperor, made a pilgrimage to the chapel, where he was healed of a serious sickness. In appreciation he authorized the city to include his imperial insignia on the civic coat of arms. To the right of the Kalverstraat is Beguine Lane, leading to the quiet and peaceful courtyard of the Beguinage, which dates to the religious women of the fourteenth century and which today is a secluded haven for the old and infirm.

At the time of the Reformation the once-free Amsterdam suffered from the cruelties of the Spanish-dominated inquisition and a few years later suffered from the equally brutal persecution by Calvinists. Many suffered during the sixteenth century, when minority religious groups were not tolerated. Menno Simons (1492–1559), the great utopian founder of an Anabaptist group later called Mennonites, ardent pacifist, and champion of freedom, visited Amsterdam in 1539. While he himself was not disturbed, his followers were persecuted soon after his departure, some being burned at the stake. These waves of terror passed, and the old freedom gradually emerged again.

Today around the dam are found the palace, residence of the monarch, and the handsomely restored New Church (Nieuwe Kerk). The latter, dedicated to St. Catherine in 1408, contains some good carvings, remnants of ancient stained glass, and various monuments of historic significance, since the church was the traditional scene of the Dutch coronations.

Amsterdam remains one of the great art centers of Europe. The famous Ryksmuseum contains major works of Dutch and Flemish painters as well as those of masters of Italy and Spain. Amsterdam is, above all, the home of Rembrandt van Rijn (1606–1669), Holland's supreme artist whose paintings and etchings have greatly enriched western culture. So many are his wonderful drawings and paintings of New Testament subjects that the entire life of Christ can be reconstructed from them. This has been done beautifully by certain art critics who are appreciative of Rembrandt's mystical genius. Deeply religious, although not in the orthodox sense, Rembrandt could see the life-giving spirit in back of things. He had read the books of Jacob Boehme and the old occultists and had understood their approach to hidden truth. He was influenced, too, by the simplicity and love shown by the Mennonites, especially by his friend Pastor Cornelius C. Anslo, a powerful preacher of Amsterdam. Although Rembrandt was Protestant and esoteric, he appreciated the old Catholic tradition as well as that of the Hebrew prophets and that of Buddha. An ineffable aspect of truth comes through strongly in his New Testament drawings and paintings, especially in such works as *Jesus and the Samaritan Woman, An Angel Appears to the Shepherds*, and *Jesus Healing the Sick*. Very often one can see and feel in the mystic patterns and symbols that which links us with the other world.

The Rembrandt house, at 4 Jordenbreestraat, is fascinating to visit and can help prepare one to appreciate more fully some of the artist's works in the great galleries. He lived there from 1639 to 1658, and the house contains many of his engravings and etchings.

The tradition of religious, political, and intellectual freedom is felt as one becomes aware of some of the great souls associated with the history of Amsterdam. Dirck V. Coornhert (1522–1590), engraver, scholar, humanist, advocate of primitive Christianity, and champion of liberty, was born there. He influenced the Collegiants, who followed Christ's law of love in their pacifism, their devotion to the poor, and the healing of the sick. They considered themselves an invisible and interim church, and they clustered for many years in Amsterdam and other Dutch towns. Coornhert also influenced Jacobus Arminius (1560–1609), the great theologian who taught freedom of choice and universal redemption. Arminius preached in Amsterdam for some years and was professor at Leyden. Arminianism became the dominant theological basis for the worldwide Wesleyan tradition.

On his first visit to Amsterdam in June 1738, John Wesley wrote in his *Journal:* "The exact neatness of all the buildings here, the nice cleanness of the streets (which, we were informed, were all washed twice a week), and the canals which run through all the main streets, with rows of trees on either side, make this the pleasantest city which I have ever seen."[1]

The West Church, on Prinsengracht, was built in the early seventeenth century and is a fine structure, with a beautiful tower and great bells. Very near this church, at 263 Prinsengracht, is a house, the story of which makes for a dark page in that long history of religious liberty so extolled by the great seventeenth-century Portuguese-Jewish philosopher, Baruch Spinoza, who was born and lived in Amsterdam. That dark page was World War II during the early 1940s and the German occupation of Amsterdam, when large numbers of Jews were deported against the protest of their Dutch neighbors. The house is called the Anne Frank house, where a Jewish family lived in hiding and where the teen-age girl Anne kept a remarkable diary describing her experiences during those tragic times. It is rightly called a shrine today, and the house is a center for visiting youth from all nations.

Within sixty miles of Amsterdam is *Zwolle,* with its thirteenth-century Great Church, and a little more than a mile beyond is St. Agnes' Hill, forty feet above the plain. On the site of an old monastery there a remarkable spiritual group known as the Brethren of the Common Life sprung up. One of the world's greatest spiritual classics, *Imitation of Christ,* came from this group. Gerhard Groote (1340–1384) and Thomas a Kempis (1379–1471) are the two who were probably most responsible for the writing and editing of this work, which is still published in many languages. A few miles from Zwolle

[1] John Wesley, *The Journal,* Curnock Edition, 8 vols. (London: Epworth Press, 1938), 2:5.

is Deventer, also associated with this same spiritual group. In later years such men as Nicholas of Cusa, René Descartes, and Erasmus spent time here in meditation and study.

Utrecht, a former Roman settlement where St. Willibrord came in 696, is only twenty-five miles south of Amsterdam and is easily reached by rail or road. The majestic cathedral there has a belfry of 376 feet, the highest in Holland. Only ten miles west of Amsterdam is Haarlem, with the great fourteenth-century Church of St. Bavo. The church has one of Europe's finest pipe organs, played by Handel and Mozart in earlier times and used for services and concerts today. The splendid Frans Hals Museum is there, too, with works by Hals and other Dutch artists.

Tips for Travelers

In Amsterdam the Parkhotel is a very lovely place to stay; it is well-located at number one Hobbemastraat. The Ryksmuseum is a short walk in one direction and in another is the Leidesplein. A few steps from the hotel is a dock where one can take a boat for the canal trip, which is perhaps the best way to be introduced to the delights of Amsterdam.

At the Leidesplein, near the Opera House, is the American Hotel, a spacious castle-like structure and also a good place to lodge or to dine.

Canal trips, usually lasting from one to two hours, run both during the day and in the evening. Many of the towers, notable buildings, and bridges are illuminated, adding charm to the evening trips.

From the Central Railway Station, excursions can be made to a variety of interesting places, such as the fishing village of Volendam or to Haarlem, Utrecht, or more distant points.

SCANDINAVIA

In ancient times when the Scandinavian lands were ruled by the devotees of the old gods, there lived a great giantess called Gefion. Sometimes she has been identified with the goddess Freyja. In her desire for more land she went to see the Swedish king, Gylfi, who offered her all the land she could plough in one day. Gefion had four sons, whom she turned into big oxen, and they ploughed all the land around Zealand until it was separated from Sweden and became an island. This is Denmark. A wonderful fountain with statuary depicting the giant goddess and her oxen sons, done by Anders Bundgaard in 1908, is a chief sight along the Langelinie, the lovely promenade of today's Copenhagen. Not far away is the bronze figure by Edvard Ericksen of the Little Mermaid, from the fairy stories of the beloved Hans Christian Andersen (1805–1875). The Little Mermaid remains the universally recognized symbol for Copenhagen.

Something of the charming fairy story atmosphere is reflected in the delightful Tivoli Park, across from the entry of which is a fine statue of a happy Hans Andersen. The city is widely known both for these lighter aspects, including the famed Schumann Circus, as well as for its splendid museums. The National Museum includes a remarkable prehistoric collection and outstanding arctic exhibits. The Ny Carlsberg Glyptothek is a place not to be missed, with its beautiful interior containing superb statuary from various backgrounds, including works from Greek and Roman periods.

The Thorvaldsen Museum is distinctive and holds many

works by Denmark's most celebrated and loved sculptor, Bertel Thorvaldsen (1770–1844), whose grave is in the courtyard. The museum is on a canal by the vast Christiansborg Palace, where the twelfth-century bishop's residence once stood.

Known as early as 1043 as "Havn," Copenhagen had no doubt been a settlement many years earlier. Tacitus, the Roman historian, tells of how the Earth Goddess Nerthus traveled around Denmark in a sacred wagon, drawn by oxen. Havn was probably a part of that legendary itinerary. Bishop Absalon of Roskilde built a residence here in the twelfth century, when the town was already known by its present name. The Church of Our Lady, now the Cathedral of Copenhagen, probably dates to this period. It was rebuilt along neo-classical lines in the early nineteenth century and has been Lutheran since Reformation times.

The cathedral is just north of the market in the old city. Of special interest are the splendid marble sculptures of Christ and the apostles, and the angel baptismal font by Thorvaldsen. This majestic statue of the Redeemer in the act of blessing is probably the best known and most copied statue of the Protestant world.

The Church of the Holy Ghost is an inspiring place to enter. While the present building reflects major rebuilding after a fire, the old foundations remain, and vibrations from continuing worship since the fourteenth century can be felt. The old medieval building adjoining the church had been a convent in earlier centuries. The Church of the Redeemer, also called Our Saviour's Church, in the Christianshavn section, has a beautiful baroque altar and an unusual tower 305 feet high, with an outside staircase.

Near the cathedral and in the area of the university, the latter founded in 1478 by King Christian I, is St. Peter's Church and an historic synagogue. A little north of the synagogue is the Trinity Church, with the famous Round Tower that was built in 1642 as an observatory. Inscribed on the tower are the words: "Direct, oh Lord!, wisdom and justice in the heart of the crowned king, Christian IV." These churches in the old city

124

were built on still earlier places of worship, some going back to pagan days.

As Thorvaldsen and Andersen are a vital part of Copenhagen's life, so, too, are Grundtvig and Kierkegaard. Nicolai F. S. Grundtvig (1785–1872), pastor, theologian, historian, hymn writer, poet, and a most influential figure in the life of both the church and society in Denmark, was a staunch friend of freedom who gave a new interpretation of the old Norse mythology as it blends with the Christian faith and practice. Northwest of the city, beyond the Botanic Gardens on a high plateau, stands the imposing Grundtvig Church, built in 1921–1940, in memory of the noted theologian. Soeren Kierkegaard (1813–1855), profound religious thinker and author, spent his whole life in Copenhagen. While scarcely recognized in his rather brief lifetime, his theology became a major influence throughout the world a century later.

About twenty miles west of Copenhagen is the ancient town of Roskilde, where the old king Harold Bluetooth built a wooden church around 960 and where later the red-brick cathedral was built. Here are the tombs of the Danish monarchs.

Odense, the capital of the Island of Funen, is an ancient town named for Odin, the old Nordic God. Hans Christian Andersen's childhood home is here, as is a fine thirteenth-century Gothic Cathedral of St. Knud. A fairytale atmosphere permeates some of the Danish countryside on the way to Odense. In still another direction, north of Copenhagen, is Helsingør, the Elsinore of Shakespeare's *Hamlet* and a seaport where boat-trains cross the waters to Sweden. The picturesque Kronborg Castle is associated with the ghost in *Hamlet* which is performed here on occasion. A statue of Denmark's guardian spirit is on the casements.

Tips for Travelers

The Scandinavian cities have some excellent mission hotels, which are under the direction of a branch of the church. They are comfortable and clean, often as attractive as regular hotels, and more reasonably priced. Strong drinks are not served. Copenhagen has several such hotels. We have stayed at the Missionshotellet, Løngangstraede 27, which is well-located and has neat, well-appointed rooms and good food.

Copenhagen can be especially appreciated on foot when seeing the old section. A map of the city is always a good aid. Good motor coach excursions will save both one's feet and time. All-day trips are available to see Odense, the castle country, and others by boat go to the Swedish port of Malmo.

STOCKHOLM

A beautiful city on a group of islands, Stockholm is at the junction of Lake Mälaren with an inlet of the Baltic Sea. From early times the old gods were worshiped in what is called today Stockholm and Sweden. While archeological excavations reveal a few aspects of the old religion, psychical research and mystical experience is necessary to catch the authentic spirit of the ancient faith and practice. Whether in Stockholm or Uppsala, or Vadstena, the oldest churches were usually built on ground sacred to the ancients. Wooden temples of worship were erected by the old religionists prior to the gradual introduction of Christianity. Sometimes a quiet period of meditation in one of the old churches will reveal thoughts, feelings, and inward pictures of what had gone on at that place in earlier times. In Scandinavia the Earth Deities were widely worshiped, often in places corresponding to certain undersurface telluric energies, so that today's pilgrim may suddenly feel such powers, having an experience of being on holy ground.

In the oldest part of the city is the Great Church of St. Nicholas, the Cathedral of Stockholm. It is on the island of Staden, just beyond the vast Royal Palace, residence of the monarch's family. This church has a very lovely altar, a beautiful pulpit, and fine carvings including that of St. George and the Dragon. Parts of the church date to the thirteenth century. Nearby on the island is the Church of St. Gertrude, also known as the German Church, dedicated to the revered visionary and healer unto whom intercessions have been made for centuries. Winding one's way along narrow lanes one finds a bridge to the little island of Riddarholmen, on which is the Riddarholms Church. The origin of the church goes back seven centuries, and at one time it was connected with the monastery of the Grey Friars. Here are the graves of the kings and queens of Sweden.

The visitor in Stockholm will want to see the handsome City Hall, which is an outstanding example of modern architecture built in 1911-1923. It is located on what is called the King's Island, and its great tower of 348 feet rises above the waters of Lake Mälaren as a major symbol of the city. Another worthwhile visit is to go to the National Museum. This is reached from the Gustav Adolfs Torg by passing the spectacular Grand Hotel to the south end of the peninsula. The gallery contains works of such masters as Rembrandt and Rubens as well as those of modern Swedish artists including the great Anders Zorn (1860-1920). Many of the latter's works, especially those depicting the people and folk lore of Delacarlia, may be seen in the Zorn Museum at Mora, in central Sweden.

St. Birgitta (c. 1303–1373), or Bridget, is probably the best known of the Swedish saints. She was the mother of eight children, and after her husband's death she devoted herself to religious work, founding the Order of the Holy Saviour chiefly for women. While her work was carried on throughout Sweden as well as in Rome, where she spent her later years, the mother house is in Vadstena some 150 miles southwest of Stockholm. Birgitta was a remarkable visionary and religious reformer and was called heretical by her critics. Her prophetic utterances are contained in her book called *Revelation.* Especially known for her healing ministry, Birgitta is still invoked for curative blessings.

One of Stockholm's greatest native sons is Emmanuel

Swedenborg (1688–1772), the great philosopher, scientist, metaphysician, and mystic. The author of many books, he developed from his visions the basic idea that the physical and spiritual worlds are in close harmony, each natural phenomenon shadowing a spiritual reality. His followers founded the Church of the New Jerusalem. Swedenborg spent some years in London. Once he wrote to John Wesley saying he had been informed from the spirit world that Wesley wanted to meet him. This was true, and Wesley replied, setting a time when he would arrive in London. Swedenborg responded in a letter saying he would be departing this life before that day (which he did) and that they would have to meet later on the other side. More than a century later, his body was removed from London at the request of the Swedish government and was taken to the Cathedral at Uppsala.

One of the great heathen temples built of wood still stood at Old Uppsala at the end of the eleventh century, indicating how late Christianity came to Sweden. On this sacred ground a Christian church was built in the early twelfth century. Interestingly enough, the old temple was that of Freyr, the God of Light, and the new church was that of Christ, the Light of the world. We see a blending of certain pagan and Christian ideas in their mutual reverence for light. Old Uppsala, or *Gamla Uppsala,* is three miles north of the noted university center and Protestant archbishopric city of Uppsala, which is forty-five miles above Stockholm. The thirteenth-century cathedral has been the scene of important ecumenical events, and is the burial place of Archbishop Nathan Soderblom (1866–1931), the Protestant theologian, peacemaker, and world leader in the movement for church unity.

The Stockholm area is rich in historic and religious background, and whether one's interest is in the old religion or the Catholic or Protestant, or in seeing the relation of all of them to the realm of worship, the area has much for the pilgrim to explore.

A boat trip on the canals is a good way to view Stockholm, or an hour's trip by steamer will take one to Drottningholm, the royal summer palace on an island in Lake Mälar. The railroads are excellent for longer journeys.

The Grand Hotel, S. Blasieholmshammen 8, is elegant and expensive; the Continental, Klara Vatturgränd 4, is a large first-class hotel opposite the central station, and the well-located Strand, Nybrokajen 9, has a good reputation.

OSLO

Whether one approaches Oslo by rail, road, or water, entering this oldest of the Scandinavian capitals and most spacious of cities is an exciting experience. Located at the north end of the lengthy Oslo Fjord and at the base of wooded hills, the city is full of beauty and evokes a sense of mystery.

Probably a small landing place in pre-Christian times, it was established by King Harold Hårdråde in 1050 as a city, with a bishopric and a cathedral coming a generation later. Approaching Oslo by boat on the fjord, one sees on the right the grim old castle of Akershus, which dates to the thirteenth century. Immediately beyond the piers looms the most commanding landmark of the city, the great City Hall. This modern structure, erected between 1931 and 1950 and designed by Arnstein Arneberg and Magnus Poulsson, is the most impressive rådhus I have ever seen. Statuary and fountains on the spacious grounds surround the building, and it has two great towers, one containing a fine carillon of thirty-eight bells.

The main entrance from the courtyard, facing Nansen's Place rather than the fjord, has a beautiful cascaded fountain above which is a huge astrological clock. On the three canopied walls surrounding the courtyard are wonderful multi-colored reliefs inspired by the old Norse mythology. One meets the Goddess Frigg and the God Tor, the Giants and the Norns who are the forces of good caring for the holy tree, the Valkyries disguised as swan-maidens, the eagle atop the ash tree, and the guiding ravens. These and the others are there in a great saga of life, and this is before one even enters the City Hall. In the central hall and along the massive staircases are frescoes illustrating the history of Norway from early times to the mid-twentieth century, including the times of the heroic King Haakon VII. Symbols of the old Norway and the Christian faith abound. Every gallery and meeting room throughout the huge building is characterized by special art works, frescoes, statuary, vast murals, and tapestries. The Munch Room has a painting of *Life* by the famous Norwegian artist Edvard Munch (1863–1944). One should allow several hours for viewing this amazing building, which re-echoes some of the timeless emblems of Nordic life and faith.

Karl Johansgate is the main thoroughfare, leading from the east railway station to the Royal Palace. Oslo also has the Market Place, the Torvet, which opens out to the north and from where one can see the Cathedral of Our Saviour. Built on ground long considered holy, the present structure dates to 1697 and contains many art treasures of both the past and of the twentieth century. Associated with this church in early times is the name of St. Hallvard (d. 1043), who is said to have rescued a woman who was falsely accused of stealing. Both he and the woman were killed by the pursuers. People called him a martyr because he died in defense of the innocent. Hallvard's body was later placed at the cathedral in Oslo, and he came to be considered the patron saint of the city.

I will never forget that when my wife and I were delegates to the World Methodist Conference in Oslo, the spiritual vibrations were very strong while we were gathered in an ecumenical service in this cathedral. Lutheran and Catholic clergy met with us, and with more than fifty nations represented in the sanctuary, lines of division seemed to miraculously vanish in the feeling of kinship with one another and with the celestial hosts.

Farther along on Karl Johansgate is the Grand Hotel, where it is said that in his later years Henrik Ibsen (1828–1906), the great dramatist, could be seen late every afternoon as he sat for awhile in one of the dining rooms. A short distance away is the National Theatre, where fine statues in the front honor both Ibsen and Björnstjerne Björnson (1832–1910), the Norwegian poet, dramatist, and social reformer.

The Royal Palace, though modest in size, is attractively situated on a hill at the head of the street. The popular King Olaf is sometimes seen mingling with his people on the streets of Oslo.

The city has a good National Gallery comprising works by the famous old European masters as well as those by the more modern Scandinavian artists such as J. C. Dahl, Edvard Munch, and Anders Zorn. The center of the university is near the palace, although the "student town," housing most of the students, is in Sognsvei, a few miles north of the city.

Trinity Church, with its fine stained glass and its very old organ, St. Olaf's Church, and the Old Akers Church, mentioned as long ago as 1150, are of special interest. Opposite St. Olaf's is the Kunstindustri Museum, which contains the twelfth-century tapestry from the Baldishol Church in Hedemarken.

No visitor would want to miss Frogner Park, in the northwest section of Oslo, and the Vigeland Gardens. Here are the famous and controversial statues by Gustav Vigeland (1869–1943), the great Norwegian sculptor who spent more than forty years creating out of stone, iron, and bronze the hundreds of larger-than-life human forms that portray all phases of life from infancy to old age, with the overtones of eternity. There are 150 sculptural groups. The central tall monolith, made from a single stone block, consists of 121 intertwined bodily forms. Fifty-eight bronze groups are on the Vigeland Bridge, as is the noted "Wheel of Life." All of these nude bodies so marvelously carved are an amazing sight. The gardens enclosing the statuary consist of eighty acres. One must see the Vigeland work to appreciate the gigantic scale upon which it was done.

About seven miles northwest of the city center on a lovely wooded hill is the Holmenkollen Ski-Jump, where there is a restaurant and a museum, with a fantastic view of Oslo and the surrounding area.

Another fascinating area to see is Bygdøy, which may be reached by motorboats from the pier in front of the City Hall. There is located an open-air folk museum, with buildings housing the ancient Viking ships. These had been excavated early in the twentieth century and had been used as burial vessels in the ninth century. One is sixty-eight feet long and sixteen feet wide in the middle. Later vessels include the arctic ship Fram and the balsa wood raft Kon-Tiki, in which Thor Heyerdahl and his companions sailed from Peru to the Polynesian Islands in 1947.

Bygdøy also has typical houses of earlier times brought in from the provinces, as well as objects of religious art, and such unusual treasures as Ibsen's study. The old crafts are practiced here, and one sees many participants in their colorful, traditional dress. Most fascinating of all to the pilgrim is the twelfth-century stave church from Gol brought to Bygdøy in 1885. Less than thirty of these rare old wooden churches of the early medieval times are still in existence in Norway. More than anything else, the churches reflect in their mysterious symbolism the wonderful blending of the old religion and Christianity.

Tips for Travelers

The Grand Hotel, Karl Johansgate 31, is a charming place, and its dining room is excellent. The Stefan Hotel, Rosenbrantzgate 1, is a pleasant and moderately priced hotel, with good food. The Ansgar Misjonshotel, Mollergaten 26, is a comfortable mission hotel. During summer months, the Student Town of the University, a few miles out of the city but with rapid train service, is used as a hotel. It is called the Studenbyens Sommerhotel and is at Sognaveien 85.

Plan to see the Oslo Fjord by boat, and consider an all-day trip to the mountains, perhaps Norefjell, which is a lovely area of woods and lakes and the site of some of the Olympic ski meets. An all-day or overnight excursion could be made to the Heddal Church, largest of Norway's old stave churches dating from the thirteenth century. Exciting three-day tours can be made by motor coach and Sognefjord steamer from Oslo to Bergen via Fragerness, Lake Tyin, the rugged Jotunheimen mountains, Borgund with its stave church, Stalheim, and Voss.

BORGUND

The remaining stave churches of Norway are among the real wonders of Europe. In the valleys among the wooded hills and mountains where the twenty-five to thirty historic structures still appear, they seem an integral part of Mother Earth, as if constructed by master workmen whose spirits were as one with the Deity. The mounting levels of roofs with the spreading symbols, like branches of a tree, rise up from the holy ground. No example is more inspiring than what the expectant pilgrim finds at Borgund.

When the Christian Gospel was brought to Norway in the early eleventh century, places of worship for the old religion were in the woods and in temples made of timber with symbolic carvings. The stave churches were erected along similar lines. Some scholars feel that the interior plan came from early churches of England, but this was for liturgical purposes. The basic construction is that of the old Norway.

The Borgund Church was built around 1150 and dedicated to St. Andrew. Practically unchanged, the church is today one of the oldest timbered buildings still standing in the world. It is an exciting and awe-inspiring sight to arrive in the valley, with wooded hills above, and to approach the church, partially surrounded by a graveyard, and with a strange old belfry a short distance away. An increasing spiritual power is felt in each step one takes toward the church. For me it became so strong that I

133

knew I stood on holy ground that evoked great emotions of reverence and awe.

The various superimposed roofs, each steep and shingled, have a well-planned purpose. The lowest part helps to protect the partly open section encircling the structure from the elements. Each roof has its perfect place in the plan. Because no glass was used in that early time and in that remote place, the tiny apertures let a bit of daylight into the interior. The strong columns or "staves" are seen extending through the walls, and the gables have the old dragon-heads and crosses on them. A slender spire pointing toward heaven extends above the uppermost roofs. The doors are beautifully decorated with carvings, especially the west portal with its entwined serpents. The origin of these unusual designs obviously goes back to pagan times. Runic inscriptions help to date the building.

Going inside, one is stirred by the remarkable design and strength of the building. The main support is the rectangle of staves dividing the central nave area and the surrounding lower aisles. These huge staves, which are polished pine trunks supporting the main roof, are held together by pairs of horizontal planks in the form of St. Andrew's Cross. The building has been made entirely of hard pine, selected by those master craftsmen of yore and treated in a secret way now unknown that gives the timber unusual strength. The building is so strong and flexible that it has withstood more than 800 years of the severe mountainous climate of Norway. Not a single piece of metal has been used in it. Surely the builders were acquainted with an esoteric tradition to have built such a structure that not only still stands in its singular beauty but still evokes the blessings of the Spirit.

Some of the interior fittings for the choir and altar area have been long missing. In the past many candles were used in the Christian worship, and at the altar the brightest array of candlelight would focus on a panel of scenes from the life of Christ and Mary. Tapestries were used to encircle the central rectangle of the nave. A sixteenth-century pulpit remains, as does a slightly later altar piece. Hidden on the walls of the interior are many runic inscriptions and carvings. St. Andrew's stave church in Borgund is a perfect place for a true pilgrimage.

Some lovely and deeply cherished primitive art has come from the stave churches; some of the works are still seen in the sanctuaries today, and other pieces are in museums. The churches have some exquisite altar frontals and paintings on wood, which often portray the Virgin Mary, around whom medieval Nordic artists and poets focused their devotion. In some stave churches the ceilings are painted with scenes from the life of Christ and Mary and from stories of the old heroes and saints.

The old Norse folklore persists, and wherever there is mention of the giants and the little people, the trolls and the nisser, there is an indelible link with the presence of nature spirits. The fairy stories are picturesque and may be given to exaggeration, but the deeper truth in them is always present. Norway has a great heritage in the supernormal. Rudolf Steiner, the German scholar and philosopher, tells of how he found the answers to some of life's deepest mysteries by listening to the counsel of a Norwegian woodland spirit.

North of Borgund lies the greatest mountain range of northern Europe, the Jotunheimen, with peaks of seven and eight thousand feet. It is the area of the frost giants, after whom the mountains are named. Lake Tyin is in this rugged section, and here the surrounding mountains are often snow-covered even in mid-summer. Further west is the Horunger, believed by many to be the grandest group of mountains in the whole mighty range, with its many glaciers. A trip through this majestic country is exciting, and the scenic wonders increase as one descends the mountains toward Sognefjord, the largest of the great fjords. A steamer carries one along the deep blue waters, with mountains rising on either side and with literally hundreds of waterfalls from the glaciers and springs above. From where the boat docks for Stalheim, a coach takes one up a series of hairpin curves to one of the most spectacular views of Europe. From the promontory at the Stalheim Hotel can be

135

viewed the wonders of deep valleys far below, and towering mountains and multi-colored skies above, making a symphony of praise to the Creator. Up the path a short distance from the mountain hotel is a monument to Kaiser Wilhelm II, for whom unspoiled Stalheim was a favorite holiday place for some twenty summers.

The mountainous lands of the giants and the great fjords reaching in from the coast make this area of Norway wonderful to visit. The marvels and mysteries combined in such a world of contrasting beauty and enchantment seem miraculously gathered up in Borgund as one enters the old stave church for reflection and worship.

Tips for Travelers

Many fine mountain inns are located in the Jotunheimen and the Sognefjord areas and on the way to Borgund. The hotel on Lake Tyin and the Stalheim Hotel at Stalheim are excellent and are included on some of the three-day tours between Oslo and Bergen. About twenty miles west of Borgund is the picturesque town of Laerdal, on a river famous for its salmon. There is the Lindstrøm Turisthotel which serves fine fresh fish meals and is a convenient center for lodging.

BERGEN

Located in the heart of Norway's fjord country, Bergen is beautifully situated on the western coast. The waters of the North Sea inlets form an ideal harbor, with wooded mountains rising as the eastern background. At one time Bergen had been the capital, a favorite city of the medieval kings, and an important port of the famous Hanseatic League. Bergen is still one of the major harbors of Scandinavia, a prosperous center for seafarers and fishermen, as well as a distinctive place of culture and the arts.

A settlement was located there long before the eleventh-century kings, for the area has the marks of the early Vikings and the reminders of an ancient religion. In European history Bergen became widely known in the Middle Ages when it had become a part of the Hanseatic League, that influential German mercantile group that promoted trade across the northern regions of the continent and in the great ports from Britain to Sweden. The league exercised a widespread control over commerce for four or five hundred years. At today's harbor in Bergen, the old quayside is still full of color and activity, the medieval wooden warehouses reconstructed after fires now used for craftsmen and artists and for workshops and stores. The oldest of these gabled buildings along the harbor's shore is the fascinating Hanseatic Museum. It is furnished in the manner of the sixteenth century, showing something of the daily life of the Hanseatic merchants and their apprentices and containing many documents and other items of historic interest.

There, too, at the water's edge, is the famous Torvet, the colorful market place with many fish stands and tanks where local housewives buy their fish live. All travelers from afar come there to enter the colorful scene. On the southeast side of the market is a statue of the pioneer Norwegian dramatist, Ludwig Holberg (1684–1754), who was born in Bergen.

Northwest of the wharfs will be found St. Mary's Church, a twelfth-century edifice with twin towers. This was a German-speaking church in the old days and a place of worship for the Hanseatic merchants who presented the baroque pulpit. A few blocks beyond is "Old Bergen," an open-air folk museum with a number of the old houses.

In the area immediately in back of the market place are some interesting old streets. Kong Oskar Gate leads to the sixteenth-century Church of the Holy Cross, which was founded in 1170 and carries a name that reflects the holiness of wood, both in the trees of the old religion and that of the cross of Christ. The street leads on to the cathedral, which while restored in the nineteenth century, dates to an original structure of the thirteenth century when it was attached to a monastery.

Several fine museums in the city include the Vestland Museum of Arts and Crafts, near the lovely public gardens with its monument to two of Bergen's well-loved citizens: Ole Bull (1810–1880), the famous violinist, and Edvard Grieg (1843–1907), the great composer. The Bergen Museum has a splendid folk art collection that includes some of the medieval pieces from the stave churches. In the nearby Nygard Park is Vigeland's Unicorn Fountain.

To appreciate the unusual beauty of the Bergen setting one should take the funicular to Fløifjell, in the northeast part of the city and more than a thousand feet above the water. At this place are marvelous vistas.

One of the most delightful excursions is to Trollhaugen, the home of Edvard Grieg. Built in 1884 on a wooded promontory about seven miles from Bergen, he lived there the last 22 years of his life with his wife, Nina. It is an idyllic scene overlooking a fjord and reflects the enchantment of a world of trolls and fairies and giants. We meet them all in the music of Grieg whose great passion was to portray the living mythology and folk spirits of Norway. The great Ibsen asked him to compose the music for the fantastic play *Peer Gynt,* and the haunting melodies of his lyric suite are widely loved. In the old romantic spirit, Grieg's music not only touches the heart but arouses anew the deep faculties of mystical perception. A Parisian critic called him "the living, thrilling incarnation of Norway." At today's summer musical festivals, people gather on the green lawns around the villa of Trollhaugen, while the windows are wide open, and guest artists play these melodies on Grieg's piano.

Nearby is the twelfth-century Fantoft Stave Church, which was built so long ago in the little village of Fortun at the head of Sognefjord. In the late nineteenth century when a new church was built in that village, an appreciative Bergen citizen had the stave church transported and reconstructed in its present beautifully situated place. It blends perfectly with the woods and soil where it now stands, as if providentially placed to correspond with the telluric energy lines of Mother Earth. In the chancel are the fine medieval wooden figures of St. John and St. Peter. The opening in the wall of the chancel is believed to be a lepers' window through which they could follow the service, receiving the holy elements and sometimes a healing of both soul and body. On the north wall is an inscription to the honor of Mary. There, too, is a sacred green touchstone, mounted in the doorpost, touched by pilgrims through the centuries and, of today, as a transmitter of blessing. Outside on a holy mound there is a stone cross from early times. In the days before the church buildings, the people would gather around a stone cross on a mound in the woods to hear the Word and to be baptized with water from a nearby holy well. In Norway there is always a close relationship between the things of spirit and of nature.

The Røldal stave church, some miles southeast of Bergen, was a special place of pilgrimage in former times, when secret religious services were held on Midsummer Night for miraculous healings. Villagers from the Bergen area made the trek in secret. Many of the old holy places of Norway are still frequented by those who are sensitive to the meaningful vibrations, the invisible powers, and the healing energies.

Tips for Travelers

Bergen is an ideal base for seeing the great fjord country of western Norway. Many good excursions are available by boat, coach, and rail. Rapid rail service runs to Oslo, as do steamer trips through the fjords to Trondheim, where there is a lovely cathedral of historic significance. There are also flights to the land of the midnight sun on the shores of the Arctic Ocean, the home of the Laplanders.

The Norge is the leading hotel of Bergen. The Neptun, Valckendorffsgate 8, is a quiet and modest hotel, well-located, and with a good restaurant.

The Bergen International Festival, featuring music, drama, and the arts, is held annually during late May and early June.

EPILOGUE

God . . . said, . . . put off thy shoes from off thy
feet, for the place whereon thou standest is holy ground.

EXODUS 3:4-5

These words that Moses heard at the burning bush more than
three thousand years ago seem quite fitting today for travelers
who experience some of the wonders of Europe's sacred places.
Wherever we feel a divine presence or a supernal power, be it
at Iona or Borgund, in the heart of Paris or in a secluded spot
in the shadow of the Jungfrau, that place for us becomes holy
ground. Geographically and spiritually the world is full of
wonderful secrets, awaiting discovery by happy and expectant
pilgrims.

We find the earth is a living being, not only with a body
but also with a soul, and that when we travel with an open
mind and a glad spirit we are more apt to find the delights it
offers. As we enjoy the lands north of the Alps, the history, the
people, the culture, the scenery, with all the abiding values and
cherished experiences arising from the encompassing spiritual
order, we realize, too, that there is so much more to see and to
feel not only in these areas but in regions beyond.

Among the experiences that become ours in making a
pilgrimage is the awakening of certain dormant faculties of perception. We see what we had not seen before and often with
eyes for invisibles. When at a sacred place and we are inwardly
attuned with the Eternal, we sometimes find ourselves practicing the ancient doctrine of communion of saints. In such

141

inspired moments we experience freshly and meaningfully the reality of our own personal immortality.

As I have indicated in this book, we cannot move around some of these enchanting places of old Europe without having our outlook on life influenced and without being blessed at the deeper levels of our being. It is my prayer that each reader will find some insights that will help make that person's experience of travel one of pilgrimage, too.

INDEX

144